The Practitioner Inquiry Series

Marilyn Cochran-Smith and Susan L. Lytle, *SERIES EDITORS*

Teacher/Mentor

A DIALOGUE FOR COLLABORATIVE LEARNING

EDITED BY

Peg Graham
Sally Hudson-Ross
Chandra Adkins
Patti McWhorter
Jennifer McDuffie Stewart

FOREWORD BY **Carl D. Glickman**

Teachers College, Columbia University
New York and London

Conference on English
Education

National Council of
Teachers of English
Urbana, Illinois

Published simultaneously by Teachers College Press, 1234 Amsterdam Avenue, New York, NY 10027 and the National Council of Teachers of English

Library of Congress Cataloging-in-Publication Data

Teacher/mentor : a dialogue for collaborative learning / edited by Peg Graham . . . [et al.] ; foreword by Carl D. Glickman.
    p.   cm. — (The practitioner inquiry series)
    Includes bibliographical references and index.
    ISBN 0-8077-3794-1 (cloth : alk. paper). — ISBN 0-8077-3793-3 (paper : alk. paper)
    1. Mentoring in education—United States.   2. College-school cooperation—United States.   3. Group work in education—United States.   4. Language arts (Secondary)—United States.   5. Student teaching—United States.   6. Teachers—Training of—United States.   I. Graham, Peg.   II. Series.
    LB1731.4.T45   1999
    373.1102'0973—dc21   98-39674

ISBN 0-8077-3793-3 (paper)
ISBN 0-8077-3794-1 (cloth)
NCTE Stock No. 19077

Printed on acid-free paper
Manufactured in the United States of America

06 05 04 03 02 01 00 99   8 7 6 5 4 3 2 1

To Margie Michael
Mentor, Teacher, Mother, Friend

Contents

Foreword

TEACHER/MENTOR is simply a wonderful book! In one manuscript, the reader can examine how a successful teacher education program has been developed among exemplary secondary school teachers, university faculty, and the teacher candidates themselves. The book is rich in planning design, implementation, and research. There is a comprehensive range of specific actions, changes, and learnings gathered by all participants. University faculty speak of how they exchanged positions with classroom teachers and recreated their university roles at a major research institution. Classroom teachers explain how they worked through harbored antagonisms toward the "ivory tower university types," how they changed their manner of mentoring teacher candidates for a full school year, and how they opened themselves up to examining and improving their own teaching practices. The teacher candidates write of initial insecurities and growing confidence as they progressed to become reflective and responsible teachers.

Although the setting is secondary teacher education in the subject fields of language arts and English, readers can make direct applications to the development and refinement of teacher education at all levels and subject areas. It is a book about how to develop truly collaborative programs between universities, colleges, and public schools. The actual guidelines, activities, assignments, and professional problem-solving methods are all described explicitly. The breadth and practicality of this book is captured in the vivid descriptions by all the participants.

The National Commission on Teaching and America's Future reported in 1996 that half of all current educators would retire in the next 10 years and with the increasing population of students, we will need more than two million new educators in our nation's classrooms. If we are to advance the democratic purpose of schools to provide an education for more and more children so that they become valued and valuable citizens, then we don't simply need more new teachers; we need more successful and caring teachers. As one teacher candidate narrated in this book, on the first full day of assuming classroom responsibilities, her cooperating teacher came to her with a smile and the gift of a package containing supplies ranging from a stapler to Tylenol! This book is a smile and a gift to all of us—in universities, colleges, and schools—committed to a new and better generation of teachers.

Carl D. Glickman
University of Georgia

Preface

As a group of teacher educators, middle and high school teachers, and pre-service teacher candidates, we have worked for several years to create a new brand of teacher education. In retrospect, our work parallels that of many professional development school collaborations, yet we reached our insights through local work and reflection, unattached to any of the major reform movements such as the Holmes Group or the National Network for Educational Renewal. This book is our story, the story of how one group of school/university collaborators challenged the traditions and systems within which we work and how we continue to co-create spaces for professional development and student learning that enrich us all. In these pages, we share our insights as a collaborative inquiry community dedicated to enhanced learning for all participants. We realize that many teachers, teacher educators, and preservice teacher candidates are exploring similar goals, and we hope that readers will see themselves and their settings here.

In *Guidelines for the Preparation of Teachers of English Language Arts* (1996), the Conference on English Education of the National Council of Teachers of English (NCTE) reiterated its 1986 goals for teacher preparation based on models and analysis of effective teaching and on placements of student teachers in schools for observation and practice. More important, in 1996, this group added two new dimensions that undergird our work. First, teacher educators in today's complex society must "form productive partnerships" with other university faculty and school leaders. Second, teacher education programs today must provide opportunities for "prospective teachers of English to construct their own unique versions of the beginning 'English language arts teacher' . . . and [become] makers of their own teacher selves" (p. 42). We agree wholeheartedly that those who support and salute this principle are "characterized by humility on the one hand, and, on the other, by pride and respect for each student's authority over his or her own learning." We would add that the same humility, pride, and respect apply for every participant's learning—teacher, college faculty, and public school students, as well as preservice teachers.

Our experience also supports the Holmes Group's (1995) claim that "education schools that fail to ground their work in well-studied practice inhabit a make-believe land, a Potemkin village of reassuring facades" (p. 90). Our work has emerged within the traditional frameworks of six public high schools and a major research institution that expects faculty to educate large numbers of preservice teachers, conduct important research, design and teach graduate courses, and lead doctoral and master's research. Yet we believe that new approaches to collaboration can provide the basis for the Holmes Group's demand for more work, more pairs of hands, new kinds of faculty expertise, and professional development for both university and school-based faculty, while creating entree for beginners into a rich, engaging vision of the teaching profession. We fundamentally agree that "no education school should conduct research on educators or produce research for educators if it cannot provide quality professional development for educators" (Holmes Group, 1995, p. 96); we believe instead that *all* of us must be researchers, teachers, and teacher educators in communities dedicated to collaborative inquiry.

In her 1992 presidential address to the American Educational Research Association, Ann Lieberman called for schools and universities to produce a new type of knowledge, which would be "co-constructed and owned by practitioner and researcher alike" (p. 10), within a community that "educates all of us, those in the university and those in the schools, a community that expands our relationships with one another and, in so doing, our knowledge and our effectiveness" (p. 11). Lieberman's words describe Goodlad's (1988) concept of co-reform as a *"symbiotic partnership"* (p. 14) of simultaneous renewal of schools and the education of educators.

We began with these principles in 1994 when 25 high school English teachers and two university faculty came to the table to reinvent teacher education. Although we share English as our discipline, we believe that our processes, insights, projects, and questions will adapt well for our colleagues working in other subject area fields and grade levels. We *do* believe, however, that collaborations among high schools and universities present unique problems, structures, and issues that more common elementary school professional development school collaborations do not face. Our work thus contributes to the relatively limited knowledge about high school/college connections.

Our experiences as a group and as individuals may be important for others interested in reinventing themselves and establishing and maintaining co-reform partnerships between colleges of education and public school professionals at the middle and secondary levels. Therefore, in Chapter 1, we tell the story of our first year together to explore some of the risks, missteps, tensions, and successes we worked through in order to begin. Each part of the book then focuses on one aspect of the collaborative inquiry community. In Part I, we focus on mentor teacher/teacher candidate relationships. High school teachers suggest productive ways of working with teacher candidates (Chapters 2 and 3) and examine some of the very honest difficulties of sharing their classrooms with others (Chapters 4 and 5).

We turn to teacher research in Part II. Campus faculty first explain how teacher research weaves together campus and school settings in our year-long program (Chapter 6). Teacher candidates then describe productive research they have done as a class (Chapter 7), as individuals (Chapters 8 and 9), and in collaboration with a mentor teacher (Chapter 10).

In Part III, issues of the teacher candidate include weekly Think Pieces that bring school issues to campus discussions (Chapter 11), coping with a sense of failure (Chapter 12), discipline (Chapter 13), leading discussions (Chapter 14), and setting up classroom routines (Chapter 15). We envision all of these chapters as *shared* readings between mentors and teacher candidates, as spaces for safe discussions of often difficult issues, and as springboards for productive explorations of tensions and concerns in their own settings.

Part IV deals with building a collaborative inquiry community. We argue for new ways of initiating and sustaining school/university collaboration (Chapters 16 and 17). Finally, we look back over our experiences to date (Chapter 18).

We gratefully acknowledge a wide range of individuals and groups that contributed to these collaborations. Throughout this work, we have had the support of the six public schools within which we began our work: Cedar Shoals High School and Clarke Central High School, Athens, Georgia; Jackson County High School, Jefferson, Georgia; Madison County High School, Danielsville, Georgia; Oconee County High School, Watkinsville, Georgia; and Washington–Wilkes Comprehensive High School, Washington, Georgia. We also have been graciously supported by colleagues at the University of Georgia College of Education (notably Russell Yeany, Dean, and Donald Schneider, Director of the School of Teacher Education) and the Department of Language Education (especially Department Chair JoBeth Allen). The National Reading Research Center sponsored our first years of collaboration; later funding has come from the University of Georgia Coca-Cola Initiative, the College of Education, and the Georgia P–16 Initiative. All of these supporters have allowed us to attempt and sustain a more productive co-reform partnership for the benefit of the next generation of teachers and our shared students in public schools.

REFERENCES

Conference on English Education. (1996). *Guidelines for the preparation of teachers of English language arts.* Urbana, IL: National Council of Teachers of English.

Goodlad, J. I. (1988). School–university partnerships for educational renewal: Rationale and concept. In K. A. Sirotnik & J. I. Goodlad (Eds.), *School–university partnerships in action* (pp. 3–31). New York: Teachers College Press.

Holmes Group. (1995). *Tomorrow's schools of education* (Report No. 48824-1034). East Lansing, MI: Author.

Lieberman, A. (1992). The meaning of scholarly activity and the building of community (presidential address at the annual meeting of the American Educational Research Association, April 1992). *Educational Researcher, 21*(6), 5–12.

CHAPTER 1

Building Nets: Evolution of a Collaborative Inquiry Community Within a High School English Teacher Education Program

Peg Graham, Sally Hudson-Ross, & Patti McWhorter

During the summer of 1994, 25 English teachers and two university professors from the University of Georgia met to redesign teacher education. This chapter is the story of how this collaborative inquiry community began as a response to concerns expressed by mentor teachers and teacher candidates across the years. Honest explorations of initial concerns, problems, struggles, strategies, and productive tensions will invite readers into the complex process of school/university collaboration.

Our mid-sized college town of Athens, Georgia, is surrounded by the six high schools in which we began our work. Cedar Shoals and Clarke Central, two city high schools, are located in Athens/Clarke County. Jackson County High School, Madison County High School, and Washington–Wilkes Comprehensive High School rest in rural areas with very different student populations. Oconee County High School, just outside Athens, is in an area that is changing overnight from farmlands to middle-class subdivisions (see Figure 1.1). Although the rural schools are 30–60-minute drives away, Athens provides an economic base for the area. As a result, many of us—teachers and teacher educators—knew each other across the years socially, through relatives or community work, or through professional development activities at the regional educational service agency that supports all of our schools. We have taken courses in the Department of Language Education at the University of Georgia (UGA) from bachelors through doctoral degrees and have always enjoyed collegial relationships with the faculty there. As much as the university location and experience binds us together, however, relationships among school and university-based colleagues and teacher candidates emerged as

Figure 1.1. Demographic data for six participating high schools during the 1994–95 school year.

School	Number of Students	Percentage European American	Percentage African American	Percentage Other Groups
Cedar Shoals	1,590	40	53	7
Clarke Central	1,440	45	50	5
Jackson County	1,050	90	10	0
Madison County	1,096	90	10	0
Oconee County	1,214	92	8	0
Washington-Wilkes	594	41	59	0

focal points when we came together in the summer of 1994, supported by a grant from the National Reading Research Center (NRRC).

Our stated goal that summer was to build a long-term collaborative community of teachers and university faculty committed to teacher education and to teacher research as a shared world view. We saw this as a way for everyone—students, teacher candidates, high school teachers, and university faculty—to learn and grow within our secondary English education program in more democratic and reciprocal, less hierarchical and divisive relationships. In order to do so, we would have to alleviate or alter traditional tensions, barriers, and stances that had kept us apart (see Chapters 16 and 17).

We met for seven 2-hour, potluck dinner meetings from June to August. Funds from NRRC paid each teacher $750 to participate in the summer experience and to work with a teacher candidate for a full year. The grant paid for the two university faculty to teach one summer course each, and during the school year their entire teaching and research assignments were dedicated to working with the cohort of 20 teacher candidates within this project (totaling five quarter courses and four sections of student teaching supervision).

Funds from NRRC also allowed us to collect a great deal of data, which we have used in shaping this chapter and book. Data included transcribed interviews with mentor teachers and teacher candidates across the year; video- or audiotaping of summer meetings and selected campus and school classes; photocopies of dialogue journals among participants and teacher candidate research, weekly Think Pieces (see Chapter 11), and other class projects; minutes of all meetings; weekly bulletins produced by campus faculty and distributed to all participants; field notes and e-mail correspondence; and written surveys and course evaluations.

In this chapter, we begin by looking back at three problematic and fundamental issues that we had to confront as we began our work together: recognizing and redefining roles and relationships, renegotiating who owns and produces knowledge, and creating more integrated lives for our teacher candidates. Next, we explore both the missteps and the negotiations that allowed us to move on as school/university collaborators. Finally, we summarize the decisions we made that set our collaborative inquiry community in motion, ready to work with our first group of teacher candidates. The chapters that follow bring that collaboration to life.

THE QUESTIONS THAT DIVIDE

Who Am I? Roles and Relationships

In initial interviews, many mentor teachers who would be joining our group revealed that they did not know enough about the teacher education program or what was expected of them in their *cooperating teacher* roles. In the absence of clarity, they assumed they lacked the theoretical knowledge that university colleagues expected, and so they had remained silent over the years. During a March 1994 interview, Shirley Burns from Jackson County High School explained how she regarded her past role in the program: "I'd like to work more closely with the university with their teacher training, to see what they do expect, because I feel like maybe we have failed them somewhere along the way." Like other teachers involved in long-term relations with teacher education faculty, she was unsure what was expected of her. With only a vague sense of having failed her university counterparts somehow, she anticipated that participation in the new program redesign might help her to understand more fully what her role was to be and perhaps to carry it out more successfully. Tellingly, however, Shirley followed up her concern about failure to meet university expectations by registering her own complaints about university representatives meeting her expectations: "We didn't have a lot of interaction with the supervising teachers at the university. I mean, we talked with them, but when they came they would observe and they'd leave. . . . And I don't think that's right."

Very much in keeping with the way relationships unfolded for university and school colleagues, Shirley accepted responsibility for failure to meet university expectations, while simultaneously feeling dissatisfied with the way her counterparts communicated with her about her student teacher's progress or what her role should be in helping her student teacher to learn. Like many of the teachers in the newly formed collaborative inquiry group, she was polite and self-protective, which discouraged her from complaining about previous programs. For years, mentor teachers had remained silent because they rarely were asked to comment, because they felt less knowledgeable than the university supervisors, and because as "traditional" teachers, many were not sure they provided the model the university teacher educators envisioned for student teachers. Silence and compliance were more comfortable than the risk of being judged wrong by "outsiders."

Like Shirley, Fran Bullock from Oconee County High School had been involved in the teacher education program prior to this experimental program year. Some of her experiences had been very positive, but she also had had some extraordinary difficulties. For example, she had had a teacher candidate who came to school on several occasions with alcohol on her breath. The teacher candidate had not been removed from the program and eventually passed student teaching in spite of a drinking problem. However, as Fran assumed, there may have been "more than [she] knew" going on. She perceived that, unfortunately, she was not privy to any information from the university about extenuating circumstances. And like Shirley, her perceived role did not empower her to question the reasons behind the decision for the teacher candidate to remain.

Renegotiating roles and relationships among mentor teachers and university faculty would consume much of our first year together. Teachers had worked in isolation as mentors, received a student teacher 2 weeks before they were to teach, and interacted with university faculty or graduate assistants only four or five times a quarter. As a result, they literally did not know what was expected of them, even after several years of serving as cooperating teachers (Alvine, 1990; Balch & Balch, 1987; Haberman, 1983; Maeroff, 1988). At the same time, their isolation and silence had engendered repressed antagonism toward the university (Butler, Etheridge, James, & Ellis, 1989; Lortie, 1975; Rosenholtz, 1989). Some teachers perceived that those representing the university did not understand their schoolwork and did not always value their input.

Within this context, the three of us authoring this chapter—Peg Graham and Sally Hudson-Ross, university professors, and Patti McWhorter, a high school teacher for 19 years—shared a dream about how teacher education might be improved. Our shared beliefs included shifting traditional roles and power relationships, adopting teacher research mindsets, and creating opportunities for connected knowing (Belenky, Clinchy, Goldberger, & Tarule, 1986) to occur within a collaborative inquiry group of school and university colleagues.

When we three came together, each of us was playing a new role ourselves. Sally and Patti had exchanged jobs for the 1993–94 school year: Sally became a high school teacher again after 17 years as a school system coordinator and teacher educator at the university, and Patti became a member of the Language Education faculty, teaching curriculum and methods, supervising student teaching field experiences, and conducting initial stages of preparation for our collaboration with mentor teachers (see Hudson-Ross & McWhorter, 1995). In the same year, Peg was a new assistant professor at the University of Georgia after 17 years as a high school English teacher and mentor to 17 student teachers in her classroom in Iowa. Patti and Peg team taught classes at the university, and Sally welcomed their practicum students into her high school classroom, experiencing the problems and potentials created by the presence of other concerned adults working with her high school students.

Those new roles made us more sensitive to the tenuous working relations between school and university personnel. For example, our initial NRRC grant proposal in early 1993 is telling in both language and goals:

> We will select 35 master teachers of English. . . . We will design and teach a summer program. . . . We will assist teachers as they implement the model in their classrooms. . . . We will teach curriculum and methods component of professional education sequence in a school-based setting. . . . We will invite all program participants to review our findings in order to evaluate the program and to develop models and materials for teacher education and dissemination.

Clearly, "we" were still running things from the university, passing on expectations, knowledge, and traditional formats to teachers and teacher candidates. At least "we" were including "them" in data analysis and program evaluation, and the intention under this language was equality and collaboration. However, we were working in a time and place when we could not see as we would a year later.

We hoped that mentor teachers would participate with us in a collaborative inquiry community as self-renewing colleagues who modeled good and reflective practice. Realistically, many teachers had not done so for a variety of reasons. We hoped to find ways to vent and honor past frustrations, clarify and renegotiate expectations for all concerned, and reorganize so that we could work together in more productive ways. We felt we could do this by focusing not on one another but on the redesign of teacher education as a better learning site for teacher candidates.

Whose Knowledge Counts? Teacher Research and Ownership

A second problem teachers expressed in initial interviews was a great divide between the teaching worlds discussed on campus and the challenges and problems they faced in their own classrooms. Shirley Burns strongly believed that part of her responsibility as a classroom teacher was to help teacher candidates understand more about the "real world of teaching." She thought the university teacher education program should "rewrite the textbooks," which tended to describe "Utopian classrooms where there's never any problems and you're just going to go in there and everything's going to be beautiful." In her opinion, the university and its texts had not helped previous student teachers to know what they were getting into before they entered the student teaching experience.

Her comments match findings by researchers in teacher education who consistently acknowledge a felt and real tension between university and school (e.g., Greenberg, 1991; Russell & Flynn, 1992; Sirotnik & Goodlad, 1988). This pull between school and university knowledge creates an awkward space for collaboration, especially in times of educational change and pressure from outside influences. Traditionally, the university has been positioned as the developer and giver of knowledge about teaching (Phelps, 1988), as evidenced by the language of our initial grant proposal above; university researchers collect information, have time to analyze and write it up, and earn acclaim and status by publishing books and articles—often about anonymous or pseudonymed teachers who may or may not look good as a result—and then teach that information in their classes and workshops. Of course, this tension is changing as more and more teachers contribute to pedagogical innovations (e.g., Atwell, 1987) and as researchers confront past ethical issues by collaborating with teacher researchers in numerous ways (e.g., Allen, Cary, & Delgado, 1996; Allen, Michalove, & Shockley, 1993; Cochran-Smith & Lytle, 1993; Hollingsworth, 1994).

Although they may not seek out written research, teachers constantly are trying to improve their practice. Like Shirley, most teachers who agreed to join our group were eager to find ways to better serve their students; they simply lacked respect for what they perceived to be unrealistic fix-alls. Many liked having student teachers because they brought new ideas. Yet, Beth Tatum, a mentor teacher from Cedar Shoals High School, spoke of the incredible pressure and frustration teachers experience as they try to find a better way to teach:

> Our problem is we are so hungry for something that works, that we grab at everything. It's almost like, you know, the grease is on fire on the stove. Baking soda, not enough. Flour, oh, what a mess, you know.

Get the warm water running so we can clean this up and turn on the fan. We're just constantly looking for ways to make it better, and sometimes we don't think through what we're looking at.

In truth, that urgency to find "what works" can lead to teachers adopting ideas for which they lack a deeper understanding, a practice that may seem atheoretical to those in the university (North, 1987; Schubert & Ayers, 1992) and make the ideas seem unworkable in the field, prompting teachers like Fran to "try new techniques constantly." Many teachers remained frustrated by how to use new information. Said Beth prior to our project:

> I've read everything on [student] self-evaluation, I've attended every workshop and I never put it in play. . . . I'm not sure what comes after step one so I just don't know where to start. And I'm to the point now I don't want another teacher to tell me where they started. I don't care where you started, I'm going to figure it out for myself.

What Beth and other mentors like her sought was a better way of thinking about practice, one that would take into account the local nested contexts of their community, school, department, and classroom cultures, as well as their personal history as teachers. Knowledge about teaching passed on to Beth from others outside those local contexts was not sufficient to address her inquiries about teaching and learning. The concept of teacher research as a way to examine one's own practice therefore connected comfortably with Beth's world view. She and other mentors at Cedar Shoals High School were, concurrently with our project, also members of the NRRC School Research Consortium (SRC), a group of teachers supported in their efforts to learn about and conduct teacher research in their own classrooms. Their emerging experiences, confidence, and knowledge provided important foundations for other teachers. (You will hear their voices in the chapters that follow.) Ownership of classroom knowledge and privileging that knowledge in the university setting also became a centerpiece of our shared work.

What About Us? Teacher Candidates and a Need for Coherence

Finally, beyond frustrations about expectations and ownership of knowledge about teaching, school and university personnel live within very different cultures with unique demands, reward systems, and values (Brookhart & Loadman, 1992; Goodlad, 1990). If we are to prepare teachers more effectively for the future, we must find ways to bridge the gap between school and university cultures and alter conventional ways of doing business together (Darling-Hammond, 1994; Goodlad, 1990; Holmes Group, 1995; Levine, 1992; Lieberman, 1992).

Traditionally, the University of Georgia Department of Language Education has prepared secondary English teachers for grades 7–12 through field centers connecting schools and university for up to two quarters (Ellis, 1981; Veal, Ellis, Agee, Kirby, & Moore, 1976). The undergraduate B.S.Ed. is based on a strong liberal arts core and 40 quarter hours in English, linguistics, drama, and/or comparative literature in sophomore and junior years, with English education courses in language studies, literature, composition, curriculum and methods, and student teaching in the senior year. All courses in the senior year are part of the current project.

Cohort groups include both undergraduate students and modified masters students who already have the equivalent of an undergraduate degree in English. The latter students complete education requirements, further graduate courses for the master's degree, and the same full year of English education courses and student teaching that the undergraduates take. Many masters students are "mature," having returned to school after one or more years in business, journalism, or other fields.

In spite of this rich background in the content area for those entering the English education major, a review of 20 years of program and course evaluations revealed that teacher candidates were caught among competing notions of what constituted good English teaching. English education courses challenged the teaching methods and content coverage of junior-year university English courses. School experiences and mentor teachers' beliefs further complicated novices' outlooks.

We heard these student voices publicly when recent graduates initiated a forum on how to work with student teachers at our state English/language arts conference in the summer of 1993. Five former teacher candidates were highly conscious of school/university communication and theoretical gaps when they entered the field. They reported that mentor teachers ignored notes from campus, perceived a clash between campus and school philosophies, and even "scoffed" at the university. One graduate said, "Teachers would tone down my ideas considerably, but I got a taste of what I wanted to do." Subconsciously voicing teachers' fear of being judged by the university, another said:

> A lot of my expectations from school formed covertly at UGA. No one ever *said* teachers were dinosaurs, but when we read Kirby and Liner [and Vinz, 1988] and Atwell [1987], there's a covert idea that it's a sweatshop out there [in schools]. When I walked out there, I was skeptical.

Those of us on the university faculty had tinkered with the system in varied ways to meet students' demands: We encouraged August and

December 2-week field experiences at schools of their choice; we planned and talked about our courses together; we assigned a faculty member and graduate assistant to work with the same cohort of students through two quarters, including curriculum/methods and student teaching; we worked with schools to make placements earlier in the curriculum/methods quarter. However, in innumerable ways we could see only after university professors and mentor teachers had collaborated to redesign the ways we work together, we were stuck with limited visions of what the preservice experience could be, what our roles were, and how we could provide instruction.

HOW TO BEGIN?

Invitations

Patti, as a high school teacher, extended invitations to teachers in the area to join in the NRRC project to redesign teacher education. Her position as peer encouraged many teachers who were doubtful to sign on. At our initial May 23, 1994, meeting, Sally greeted 25 participants from six public high schools (2–6 from each school). "Let's try to think in completely new ways," she invited. "This does not have to look like a 'class'! It is ours to structure, plan, use for our growth as people and professionals." She explained that we three initiators of the project imagined the group working from an "emerging agenda" rather than from a preconceived "notion that somebody's going to teach us something," a long way from our original proposal. We identified "collaborative inquiry" and "teacher research" as two major themes for our shared work. Patti explained what we meant by "collaborative inquiry":

> We went with "collaborative inquiry" [as a title] because we feel like that's what it is that we want to do here. . . . These kids [teacher candidates] are coming in, and they really want answers right now. But my notion is [that when] I have a question about my teaching, there are numerous ways I can get answers for myself. And one of the most important ways I get answers is by talking to other teachers, other teachers who are well informed and who care about looking for answers and solving problems in the classroom.

Sally addressed "teacher research" by describing how teacher candidates could be assisted in becoming more independent problem solvers if they could see how we as teacher researchers formulate problems and questions for ourselves and go about looking closely at student learning, reporting carefully what we have found, and helping others to believe it is a "useful way of looking" (Lloyd-Jones, 1986).

Our overall first goal was to rewrite teacher education. Placing our concerns as teacher educators and teacher researchers on the table—both an exhilarating and a frightening stance—we invited our colleagues to do the same. In retrospect, it was important that those of us at the university opened our program and our teaching to critique first, before asking school partners to examine their own teaching. We modeled the risk taking and openness that we hoped mentor teachers and teacher candidates would take on as teacher researchers in the coming year.

Just as important, the concept of *collaborative* inquiry always combined for us a teacher research mindset with the notion of camaraderie, something our group was hungry for and that we too had enjoyed. In their introductions to the group that night, mentor teachers' end-of-year concerns poured out. They admitted that they joined the group to overcome isolation. Many felt stale or stuck in their teaching, and they wanted to be rejuvenated and avoid burnout, improve their teaching, and quit "losing kids." Roger Bailey from Oconee County High School eloquently summarized for many when he said:

> I go through great periods of time when I don't question what I
> teach—either content or technique. I'm not satisfied. What worked at
> one time doesn't surprise me any more. . . . I realize I need the society
> of my peers. We've become so insular. I see this project as a way to
> break through that. I still have my spark for teaching after a quarter of
> a century, but a new administration, book censorship, and paperwork
> are getting the best of me. (Amens from the group.) And I'm sick of
> the way I've been teaching research; I've been killing imagination in
> kids for years.

As Hollingsworth (1994) discovered, no matter what the agenda, teachers who are permitted to speak have deep and very real concerns that they want and need to discuss with peers. Our group was eager for the opportunity to work with other teachers from local schools, and we wanted their agendas and needs to be primary as we examined teaching and teacher education together. As a result of our initial, heartfelt sharing, we established three ground rules that set the tone for our summer ahead:

1. Griping and moaning are OK, as long as you're also searching.
2. All stories are welcome; we need to bring our kids in here.
3. Food is always available; help yourself at any time.

Blinders, Missteps, and, Finally, Decisions

As project initiators, we consciously wanted to turn power and leadership of this group over to the mentor teachers, believing that they had to feel completely equal from the start (or even more than equal to make up for past perceptions of inferiority). Therefore, we set only the first agenda and asked volunteers to shape, lead, and maintain minutes of future meetings. Peg and Sally took on note taking or videotaping roles that allowed them to be silent, but they often were called in to clarify, define, and guide conversation. It was hard to give up the expectation of their leadership (see Chapter 16).

As in any shared governance situation, our group initially dealt with small and safe group management decisions (how to deal with absences during the summer, given that we were being paid; how to use the two texts we had ordered; what to do with our time; how to use our own expertise and other people as resources). We charged ahead to set up small groups to list our concerns and produce a handbook and evaluation procedures—before Patti, from her unique stance, raised an important issue: "Many of our questions and concerns [and directions] come from the old model of [student teaching]. We're ready for a new model. . . . Our expectations have old baggage in them." Discussion in small groups led us to realize that "handbooks are 'done' and something 'ongoing' would be more helpful." What the mentor teachers wanted, we decided, were "parameters, not a long list of rules." We likewise rejected creating recipes and mandates for evaluating our progress and that of teacher candidates. Instead, we decided that teachers should meet throughout the school year "to discuss what is working, and how to change," that "a variety of things are possible, and what works for one does not have to work for everyone." By resisting codification, the group probably saved us from recycling past ways of working together and left the door open for future negotiations.

Gradually, we made some important decisions:

- *Placement.* A small committee of school representatives meet with Peg and Sally to review teacher candidate resumes and cover letters collected in May and make placements for colleagues from their own schools. Mentors write initial friendly letters of welcome to their candidates, and Peg and Sally send a formal letter of placement informing teacher candidates that placements are made tentatively for the entire year, not just for the traditional 2-week practicum or spring student teaching.
- *Calendar.* Teacher candidates spend the first 2 weeks of school (including Georgia's standard week of *preplanning*) with their mentor teachers at school, with Peg and Sally visiting in that setting. Fall quarter classes begin on the university calendar, and teacher candidates at first spent mornings in campus classes and afternoons at school; mornings and afternoons were reversed for winter quarter. (We quickly realized we were wearing out teacher candidates; they now meet for 4 hours 3 times a week on campus and have 2 full days at school.) Full-time student teaching occurs in the spring for 10 weeks.

- *Campus content.* Fall and winter campus curricula are team taught by Peg and Sally. They integrate language, literature, composition, curriculum, and methods, as well as emerging issues of school cultures, contexts, and issues.
- *Connecting school and university contexts.* Three-way dialogue journals (Chapter 3), teacher research projects (Chapter 6), and Think Pieces (Chapter 11), as well as other assignments, as much as possible link school experiences and practice with theory, research, and practical readings and discussion on campus.
- *Respect for school contexts.* Knowledge of and respect for each school's unique culture and context are essential to teaching well in that setting. Tact, respect, and information—rather than biases, fears, or stereotypes—must surround all discussions of and publications (including student papers) about students, schools, and communities. Assumptions must not be made about students because of where they live.
- *Mentor teacher meetings.* Large group meetings, for program input, professional development, and socialization, occur each year and across each summer (even when funding is not available). Meetings of school representatives are called as needed, but at least quarterly, to discuss issues, teacher candidates, problems, and professional development opportunities. Representatives alternate—depending on who is available on a particular night.
- *Communications.* Sally and Peg publish a weekly bulletin that lists all campus activities, syllabi, and projects, as well as news and professional development activities for mentor teachers. All participants keep in touch regularly through phone calls, e-mails, and school/campus visits.

In enacting new roles and relations with university counterparts, the mentor teachers grew to appreciate all of the options and competing perspectives voiced by the teacher group and university faculty. They understood in a deeper way how university faculty in the past had struggled with issues such as placement decisions, balancing school visits and other campus responsibilities, the burden of communicating to multiple individual sites of teacher candidate work, and teaching courses out of the context of school settings.

POSITIVE DISSONANCE: NEGOTIATING TEACHER RESEARCH AND A COLLABORATIVE INQUIRY COMMUNITY IN TEACHER EDUCATION

These decisions and a collaborative culture were not simple to achieve, however. Across our first summer, we often struggled to understand one another. One night, in particular, Peg, Sally, and Patti pointed the group back to the grant proposal, sample teacher research projects, and readings from Cochran-Smith and Lytle's *Inside/Outside* (1993) about a similar teacher education group and from Mayher's *Uncommon Sense* (1990) as a way to help us think more deeply about our teaching. Shifting the conversation from teacher education to teachers' own classrooms as sites for teacher research could have threatened the group's progress. Instead, we encountered our first genuinely productive tensions as a group and moved on to examine our roles as teachers as well as our relationships with each other and with beginners.

The opportunity arose when Chandra Adkins of Washington–Wilkes High School raised the issue of collaborative inquiry after reading the original National Reading Research Center grant proposal. (She extends this discussion in Chapter 16.) She asked Peg and Sally to clarify where our gaze would be focused as university researchers collecting data. She inquired, "I'm not sure exactly. . . . Are you investigating *our* participation in collaborative inquiry, or are you looking at what the teacher candidates are going to be doing as far as collaborative inquiry, or both, or what?" Chandra's question marked a turning point because as teachers who felt like "the low person on a totem pole," the mentors in our group needed to test our claim of seeking more equal status interactions in our proposed partnership in teacher education.

With the question posed, we had to admit to ourselves and to the mentor teachers that, yes, we *were* interested in their participation in collaborative inquiry with teacher candidates. Mentors provided sites for the field experience, and we hoped they would model an inquiry approach to teaching, perhaps learning along with their teacher candidates, as we hoped to do.

Together Peg and Sally tried to help construct a vision of teacher candidates as co-researchers supporting (and perhaps co-constructing) a teacher's goals and practices in the classroom (see Chapter 6). At various times during the meetings, we explored out loud to explain how the arrangement might benefit the mentor teacher as well as the student teacher:

> PEG: We're hoping . . . that the questions you [mentor teacher and teacher candidate] pose collaboratively are questions that—perhaps because of time constraints in the past—you really haven't been able to investigate in this systematic way. . . . This way it becomes intentional inquiry rather than something you just hit on now and then. The TC will be very useful to you . . . [and] really inform your own teaching. You need to think . . . how the whole [arrangement] can serve you.
>
> SALLY: What kinds of things would you like to have another human body in there to find out? What has happened over the years [that continues to concern or intrigue you]? . . . Now all of a sudden

you have your own researcher in your classroom who is your student teacher. With them brainstorm, "I really want to know why I
can't get kids to . . . read a book." And then you sit down and say,
"How could we find that out?" And you say, "Interview them all,"
or whatever you decide, and then the TC can *do* that for you.

Many of the mentors immediately understood how reconceptualizing
the mentor/teacher candidate relationship this way would not only serve the
teacher candidates by modeling how experienced teachers continue to learn
across their careers, but also serve the mentors' desire to think deeply about
their practice. Some teachers were also quick to appreciate how this mentor
teacher/teacher candidate arrangement as co-researchers could shift the lo-
cus of attention from judgments of teaching performances to more complex
discussions of student learning. As the school year unfolded and teacher candidates took over primary teaching responsibilities in the spring, mentor
teachers could reverse roles and become research assistants, collectors of
data rather than people saying, "You're doing this right [or wrong]."

A co-researcher role for mentor teachers was not easily embraced by
everyone. In fact, a renewed sense of mistrust and self-doubt burst forth
when Susan Little of Clarke Central High School bravely brought up her
perception from the research proposal that teachers would be placed under
the microscope. Susan had thought "the focus was totally on what happens
with the teacher candidates" and that she "was just helping you [university
teacher educators] out." But as she read the proposal and participated in the
summer dialogue, she realized that "[her] own teaching [was] . . . also being
held up for scrutiny" and she was being "asked to do a little more theoretical
kind of thinking and research than [she] had anticipated." When Peg asked
her if she felt safe enough to talk about how that realization made her feel,
Susan was able to admit she felt somewhat misled, but also confident knowing that good teachers should not be opposed to "holding their teaching up
to scrutiny."

Other voices chimed in once the floodgates of doubt were opened. One
teacher worried that she might not "fit with some of these ideas," and she
"feared the unknown." Another wondered if she would appear too uncertain
to a teacher candidate who observed her "examining [her] own teaching."
Another voiced concern that his teacher candidate might be more "current"
than he on theoretical issues, since he was "not reading the research as much
as [he] should," and he'd have to "scramble to catch up." In all cases, the
teachers did not object to trying a new role, but they were concerned with
the possibility of performing the role poorly while they were being observed
(and possibly judged) by teacher candidates and university faculty. Teachers

had had enough of that kind of scrutiny, and they didn't want to be the next group of teachers "bashed" by university researchers.

Group members attempted to work through their concerns by negotiating definitions, caring for one another's needs, and sharing personal testimony to collaboratively understand the notions of teacher research and mentoring in this new, possible configuration of their worlds and roles. In particular, Barbara Jarrard and Beth Tatum, emerging teacher researchers at Cedar Shoals High School, attested to the excitement of seeing teaching as a growing process.

Barbara reminded the mentors that teacher candidates needed classroom practice in order to make sense of the theories they investigated in the campus classroom, and the mentors would "be there to back up, to help them adjust a little," giving the traditional school/university dichotomy a new and more collaborative bent. Beth told the story of her own student teaching, which became a potent reminder to all of us about the changes we had undergone across our teaching histories. Beth exclaimed:

> When I went out to student teach, I took it on faith that the people that I was going to work with had it all under control. And then 2 years after I was on the job [in the same school], when they started changing the way they were doing things, which meant that I could no longer copy them, I got very upset at that. I felt left out on a limb and betrayed because these people that I was trying to copy because they were master teachers were changing. And nobody ever explained to me that teaching is an evolution, nobody ever explained to me that I would go through different cycles in my career. Until I figured that out, I was really angry at all these people I admired because they were changing the rules. And I see this as an opportunity for *these* teachers not to have to go through that so they can see that [learning to teach] is an evolution.

We could all appreciate Beth's story since we knew that she had done her student teaching with Patti, the teacher-leader who readily acknowledged she had fewer answers but many more questions than she had entertained 10 years earlier when Beth had student taught with her.

Roger Bailey, department chair at Oconee County High School, saw the potential for professional development in his department. He admitted that he read the proposal "from an entirely selfish view." As a teacher who was "tired of doing a lot of things the same way" and who "wanted to refurbish [his] whole program," he thought about how these new conceptualizations and roles would "strengthen the department." Roger's colleague, John Varner, envisioned their work as a "research team" of 10–12 mentors and teacher candidates who "could regularly talk" about problems that applied to their classroom. It would be a way to break their "isolation" and "talk about what truly matters and have teacher candidates there."

Without having to justify our "agenda," we watched teachers help one another to view the emerging teacher education program as an opportunity for all participants. Sally enthusiastically reiterated what we had all been trying to say:

> The world is open in this project. There are no answers, there is no way to do it, no agenda except that we will come together and try to start questioning our teaching and be gutsy enough to let a beginner come in and see that that is the way teaching should be. Not a sense of always failing . . . , but a sense of teaching as an ongoing thing.

By the end of the summer of 1994, we emerged with a vision of teacher education, professional development, and collaborative inquiry to which we had all contributed our best ideas and our deepest beliefs. In the ensuing chapters, readers will hear the voices of mentor teachers, teacher candidates, and university faculty as we tell stories of our shared experiences, insights, and struggles in the years following our initial summer meetings. In Chapter 18, we look back to examine our enactment of a collaborative inquiry culture across 4 years. With nets in place, we feel more able than ever to grow as professionals and colleagues.

REFERENCES

Allen, J., Cary, M., & Delgado, L. (1996). *Exploring blue highways: Literacy reform, school change, and the creation of learning communities.* New York: Teachers College Press.

Allen, J., Michalove, B., & Shockley, B. (1993). *Engaging children: Community and chaos in the lives of young literacy learners.* Portsmouth, NH: Heinemann.

Alvine, L. (1990, April). *An interactive, collaborative model of inservice in clinical supervision: Cooperating teachers become teacher educators.* Paper presented at the annual meeting of the American Educational Research Association, Boston.

Atwell, N. (1987). *In the middle: Writing, reading, and learning with adolescents.* Portsmouth, NH: Boynton/Cook.

Balch, P. M., & Balch, P. E. (1987). *The cooperating teacher: A practical approach for the supervision of student teachers.* Lanham, MD: University Press of America.

Belenky, M. F., Clinchy, B. M., Goldberger, N. R., & Tarule, J. M. (1986). *Women's ways of knowing: The development of self, voice, and mind.* New York: Basic Books.

Brookhart, S. M., & Loadman, W. E. (Spring, 1992). School–university collaborations: Across cultures. *Teaching Education, 4*(2), 53–68.

Butler, E. D., Etheridge, G. W., James, T. L., & Ellis, S. B. (1989, March). *Empowering teachers through collaborative mentoring designs: An empirical study.* Paper presented at the meeting of the American Association of Colleges for Teacher Education, Anaheim.

Cochran-Smith, M., & Lytle, S. L. (1993). *Inside/outside: Teacher research and knowledge.* New York: Teachers College Press.

Darling-Hammond, L. (1994). *Professional development schools: Schools for developing a profession.* New York: Teachers College Press.

Ellis, W. G. (1981). The Georgia program revisited and updated. *English Education, 13*(2), 79–85.

Goodlad, J. (1990). *Teachers for our nation's schools.* San Francisco: Jossey-Bass.

Greenberg, A. R. (1991). *High school–college partnerships: Conceptual models, programs, and issues* (ASHE–ERIC Higher Education Report No. 5). Washington, DC: ERIC Clearing House on Higher Education, George Washington University.

Haberman, M. (1983). Research on preservice laboratory and clinical experiences: Implications for teacher education. In K. Howey & W. Gardner (Eds.), *The education of teachers* (pp. 98–117). New York: Longman.

Hollingsworth, S. (1994). *Teacher research and urban literacy education: Lessons and conversations in a feminist key.* New York: Teachers College Press.

Holmes Group. (1995). *Tomorrow's schools of education* (Report No. 48824-1034). East Lansing, MI: Author.

Hudson-Ross, S., & McWhorter, P. (1995). Going back/Looking in: A Teacher educator and high school teacher explore beginning teaching together. *English Journal, 84*(2), 46–54.

Kirby, D., Liner, T., & Vinz, R. (1988). *Inside out: Developmental strategies for teaching writing* (2nd ed.). Portsmouth, NH: Boynton/Cook.

Levine, M. (Ed.). (1992). *Professional practice schools: Linking teacher education and school reform.* New York: Teachers College Press.

Lieberman, A. (1992). The meaning of scholarly activity and the building of community (presidential address at the annual meeting of the American Educational Research Association, April 1992). *Educational Researcher, 21*(6), 5–12.

Lloyd-Jones, R. (1986). The devil and research. *Kansas English, 72*(1), 4–10.

Lortie, D. (1975). *Schoolteacher: A sociological study.* Chicago: University of Chicago Press.

Maeroff, G. I. (1988). *The empowerment of teachers.* New York: Teachers College Press.

Mayher, J. (1990). *Uncommon sense: Theoretical practice in language education.* Portsmouth, NH: Heinemann.

North, S. M. (1987). *The making of knowledge in composition: Portrait of an emerging field.* Upper Montclair, NJ: Boynton/Cook.

Phelps, L. (1988). *Composition as a human science.* New York: Oxford University Press.

Rosenholtz, S. (1989). *Teachers' workplace: The social organization of schools.* New York: Longman.

Russell, J. F., & Flynn, R. B. (1992). *School–university collaboration.* Bloomington, IN: Phi Delta Kappa Educational Foundation.

Schubert, W. H., & Ayers, W. (Eds.). (1992). *Teacher lore: Learning from our own experience.* White Plains, NY: Longman.

Sirotnik, K. A., & Goodlad, J. I. (1988). *School–university partnerships in action.* New York: Teachers College Press.

Veal, L. R., Ellis, W. G., Agee, H., Kirby, D., & Moore, A. (1976). The University of Georgia teacher education program in English. *English Education, 7*(4), 218–235.

PART I

Mentor Teacher/Teacher Candidate Relationships

As a collaborative inquiry community, our relationships with each other are at the heart of our work as mentor teachers, teacher candidates, and university faculty. The most fragile of these, however, is that of the mentor teacher and the teacher candidate. When all is said and done, that relationship—its successes and its failures and how those are perceived and dealt with by all involved—becomes testimony to the ultimate success or failure of our community.

With this in mind, we begin, in Chapter 2, with our best advice about mentoring teacher candidates. From experiences across a wide spectrum of individuals and schools, this chapter provides accessible beginning points for new mentor teachers or points of discussion or thought for those more experienced. Chapter 3 presents a closer look at how a dialogue journal can connect a mentor teacher, teacher candidate, and university faculty in a meaningful discussion about teaching and learning. Their willingness to examine classroom events, students' actions and reactions, and teachers' orchestration and facilitation of learning contributes to the success of this practice—success other mentor teachers, teacher candidates, and university faculty may want to replicate.

Above all, we never fail to disclose the struggles of our work together. Chapter 4 tells the stories of mentor teachers who feel intense connections to the students in their classrooms and find it painful to let the teacher candidate take full responsibility. Their honesty in admitting the conflicting feelings of wanting to contribute to the professional development of a new teacher yet finding themselves reluctant to let go of their students provides unique insight into these complicated relationships. Finally, Chapter 5 reveals how complex the mentor teacher/teacher candidate relationship can become when a mentor teacher is forced to examine her philosophies and practice to determine whether students are really learning.

Throughout this part, as well as the rest of our book, are stories of students and classrooms across our community. Although Part I is focused specifically on the mentor teacher and teacher candidate relationship, the issues also can serve as prompts for discussion among all involved in this important work.

CHAPTER 2

Maybe Not Everything, but a Whole Lot You Always Wanted to Know About Mentoring

Beth Tatum & Patti McWhorter
with Christina Healan, Mindi Rhoades, Lillian Chandler,
Margie Michael, Andrea Bottoms Jacobson, & Amy Wilbourne

Beth and Patti join a number of their mentor teacher peers and teacher candidates to discuss what they have learned about how to be effective mentor teachers to teacher candidates. Suggestions highlight problems surrounding issues of the mentor teacher/teacher candidate relationship.

Each year, hundreds of veteran teachers agree to take under their wing college students who want to enter the profession. Being a mentor teacher can be time-consuming and emotionally draining. Nurturing and encouraging an idealistic teacher candidate is another "preparation" in a day full of lesson plans and student interactions. Our suggestions here are the result of interviews, dialogue journal entries, debriefing seminars, and the day-to-day sharing among colleagues that allows for reflection and contemplation. We will share our insights about getting started, focusing on instruction together, and, finally, reversing roles.

GETTING STARTED

Introducing the School Environment

There are many ways to make a teacher candidate, or any other visitor to a school, feel welcomed, and mentor teachers have developed different ways to do this. Christina and Margie both provide their teacher candidates with a small desk or table that becomes a teacher candidate's personal space in the classroom, an environment where space is often at a premium. Other mentor teachers greet their teacher candidates with a box of teacher supplies or goodies. Providing a new teacher candidate with space, a sense of ownership, and tools of the trade is the first way to create a sense of community.

Because an individual classroom is just a small part of the larger environment of the school, a building tour, as mundane as that may sound, is essential in order to help teacher candidates get their bearings. Introducing teacher candidates to other teachers in the building is also a way to help them feel comfortable in this new environment. Amy was pleased when her mentor teacher did not introduce her as a student teacher, but as "my new friend." This small adjustment in semantics changed the way Amy entered student teaching.

As part of the building tour, teacher candidates should be introduced to the custodial staff, school nurse, and secretaries. Support personnel can be lifesavers in an environment as unpredictable as a school, and most teachers rely on them for help and emotional support from time to time. This also broadens a teacher candidate's definitions of "faculty and staff" to include everyone on the team.

Establishing Collegial Roles

One of the most challenging problems of being a student teacher is successfully playing both roles of student and of teacher. Because of the insecurities prevalent during student teaching, the role of teacher is often difficult to assume. A mentor teacher can help provide a teacher candidate with the credibility that she needs by presenting her to students and parents as a co-professional. Margie did this with Andrea by having Andrea's space at the front of the room instead of the back. Also, all parent letters that went home the first few weeks of school contained both signatures. Both mentor teacher and teacher candidate assumed responsibilities for daily classroom procedures, as well as leading class discussions. By presenting Andrea to the class and community as a young teacher with credibility, Margie carved out a place for Andrea to grow.

In our program, teacher candidates are actively involved in preplanning activities such as preparing the classroom for the school year. Teacher candidates have painted halls, stamped books, created bulletin boards, set up computers and software, and put up posters. This gives them ownership of the space they will share with their mentors from the very beginning. Andrea found all of this effort on the part of the mentor teachers very helpful. "From the beginning, Mrs. Michael helped me ease into my new role, providing opportunities for me to taste and see the joys and challenges of teaching English."

Sharing Materials and (Gasp) Files

One of the most difficult things to share in a teaching situation is materials. In some programs, teacher candidates arrive at their designated schools with a head full of philosophy and ideas, but all about mythical students. They present a few short practice lessons to classmates on campus, but they are basically void of all teaching materials, handouts, and transparencies. If teacher candidates are going to have time to be reflective about their performance in the classroom and begin to look at teaching as a practice, they cannot spend all of their time outside of the classroom creating—from scratch—handouts, guided lessons, and examples of work. Mentor teachers can help here by opening up their files to the teacher candidate. However, this is not an easy task.

We all know that many of those folders are full of ideas pounded out on the word processor late in the night. Some of them contain evidence of lessons that were inappropriate or failed for no apparent reason and were exiled to the filing cabinet. It feels risky to open up and share this work. It also may feel unfair. "I created all this stuff," you think briefly. "My student teacher can too." However, this archeological dig into the filing cabinet tells the story of one teacher's evolution. It houses evidence of the year the school district adopted new textbooks and the board office mandated workbooks. It also reveals the time you threw out all traditional philosophies to forge your own curriculum and teaching methodologies. This glimpse into your teaching past may present you as more human and evolutionary to a teacher candidate, an important insight for beginners, and one that may cure them of seeking easy answers for all times and all students.

Encouraging Extracurricular Involvement/Observations

As teachers, we all have different roles and different teacher faces. Our demeanor may vary from class to class and with different types of student encounters. The strict math teacher might relax in her role as student council advisor as she works during an all-night lock-in to change the cafeteria into a fantasy land for a dance. And kids also have different faces for different teachers and different classroom situations. In order for a teacher candidate to see all sides of teachers and students, she needs to observe them in various settings.

One way to help teacher candidates get a holistic picture of the school is to have them attend and observe an extracurricular meeting, activity, or athletic event. This opportunity will allow them to see other sides of students. Heather, a teacher candidate, realized that Sue, a student who was quiet and reserved in English class, was a debating maniac during an Academic Bowl practice. This helped Heather to see that Sue's shyness was not a mask for insecurity, but her reaction to the environment of second-period English. It also helped Heather to begin to evaluate what was different about the English classroom and the Academic Bowl practice—differences that elicited two types of behavior.

By observing students in areas of their strength, whether football or community service, teacher candidates can begin to see the whole student and not just the student in their class. This can have a very positive impact on their teaching methodologies as well as their relationships with students. Nothing helps students feel like you have a vested interest in them more than your interest in seeing them perform outside of the classroom.

Teacher candidates also can be very helpful in extracurricular activities. Bill, a former actor, worked with students after school as they prepared performances for the Literary Fair. His previous experience gave him credibility with the students, as well as an additional experience on his resume. Other teacher candidates in our group have helped coaches, planned student writer retreats, set up after-school tutoring programs, led field trips, and established a school-wide Renaissance Fair to earn money for an English department.

Forging a Friendship with a Teacher Candidate

If the mentor teacher/teacher candidate relationship is going to expand to its full potential, there must be an underlying element of trust and friendship. If this is in place, all other conflicts of differing teaching philosophies, differing approaches to students, and different planning styles can be resolved in such a way that everyone wins and learns from the experience.

Amy and Christina are a teacher candidate/mentor teacher pair who developed a lasting friendship and partnership (see Chapter 10). They have presented their research together many times and still share teaching experiences over the phone. For Amy, this friendship developed because of Christina's little acts of kindness and consideration:

> My first real "teacher takeover" day, she [Christina] presented me with a box of my own teaching supplies—everything from a stapler to Tylenol. Talk about support! It was like being a small child on the first day of school, not knowing exactly what to expect but feeling good because you knew mom had packed your school box with everything you might need.

For Christina, forging a friendship was the most important part of the mentor teacher/teacher candidate relationship, and for this to happen, it meant spending time away from school with her teacher candidate:

Really getting to know someone often means spending time outside the school day. Amy and I were given some exceptional opportunities to build on our friendship. We attended a conference together in San Francisco, and also went to pick strawberries on a Saturday morning in the pouring rain with her two small children.

Margie and Andrea, her teacher candidate, also presented at the conference in San Francisco. When Margie's husband called the hotel to give them an update about school and family, he insisted on talking to Andrea first, telling her about all that had happened in *her* classes, for which he was subbing. Like Christina and Amy, Margie and Andrea had formed a personal relationship that also extended to their family members.

FOCUSING ON INSTRUCTION

Becoming Partners in Research and Discovery

If a mentor teacher takes time to forge a friendship with a teacher candidate and encourages a partnership between the two in the classroom, the results can be beneficial for both teachers. Taking the step to become partners in research is a leap of faith that gives both teachers a connection and investment in the teaching process that will not occur otherwise. The way to begin the dialogue is to share observations about the classes and the students. From observations, questions naturally arise. As the mentor teacher and teacher candidate begin to question together, they will find a common interest to explore as researchers.

A prime example of this took place in Patti's classroom. Patti's teacher candidate, Amy Elizabeth, had a private school background and was puzzled by the fact that some students would simply choose not to do an assignment. The students were obviously capable and the assignment not difficult. As she and Patti discussed this over the course of several weeks, Patti was able to share some of the techniques she used to get students to buy into a course. One of Patti's strengths is her ability to give students choices. She provides an environment where students can help choose the direction of the curriculum and the parameters of an assignment. However, even with all of her innovation, Patti was not able to cure the apathy that some students displayed.

Patti and Amy Elizabeth decided that they wanted to look further into the puzzle, and a research project was born. Over the course of several months their action research project took shape. It was important to both teachers, so Patti did not see it as an intrusive assignment born out of the

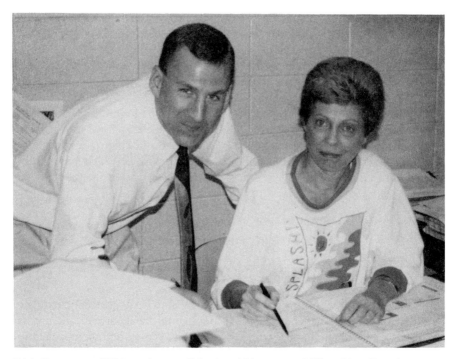

Rick Rasmussen (1998 teacher candidate) and his mentor, Lillian Chandler, plan collaboratively.

university curriculum. And because Amy Elizabeth was genuinely interested in the topic, she had an innate curiosity and energy to invest in the project. Their research consisted of talking to their classes, interviewing individual students, and sharing observations with other teachers. Although they may not submit their findings to a scholarly journal, they have shared their experience as co-researchers and the conclusions of their project with other teachers in formal conference settings.

Modeling Teacher Thinking and Behavior

Modeling is a big part of a mentor teacher's job. As mentor teachers teach and interact with students, they are illustrating for the teacher candidate a way of working the craft. Mentor teachers should, however, take the modeling a step further and render visible the thinking and the evolving philosophy of a teacher.

    One of the first things Bill found himself doing as a teacher candidate was listening to Beth talk. Before a class, Beth would take time to talk through the lesson. She explained what she was going to do and how she and the students got to this point together. Beth also discussed how she previously approached the assignment or topic differently and how other teachers in the department might do it differently. She verbalized the outcomes she hoped to observe as she and the students worked through the lesson. This type of background information kept Bill from watching the lesson in a vacuum. It allowed him the opportunity to see how a course and a teaching approach evolve.

Beth sees a very personal benefit from these prelesson conferences for classes with a teacher candidate:

> I have found that these prelesson talks really help me to focus. Many things that teachers do are the result of unspoken experiences and gut instinct. I wish I had someone to listen to me every day. It helps to put things into a perspective that can be *verbalized* and not just *felt* on a level of intuition. Often I have something that I want the teacher candidate to watch for specifically, such as the students' responses, the time students spend on a task, which students I tend to call on most, or which students tend to pull me to their desks. This gives me another set of eyes and ears to help me see and hear my classroom more accurately.

Showing teacher candidates up front that teaching is an evolutionary process can do much to dispel the notion that teaching emerges from one definitive set of rules and procedures. Mindi also feels that it is important to show teacher candidates that she continually learns about teaching:

> I am still trying to learn and improve on the same things a teacher candidate is—classroom management; lesson planning; organizing; how to teach a topic/lesson/idea; how to test or check for learning, understanding, growth, or effort; and what and how to evaluate. I am still very excited about teaching as a profession and am enthusiastic about the possibilities in education.

She models an outlook we hope all beginners will share.

Videotaping Yourself

One of the best ways to help teacher candidates become reflective teachers is to have them videotape classroom activities. In order to fully understand how intimidating and humbling (yet effective) this activity is, mentor teachers should take the time to videotape themselves. With a camera, teachers are suddenly students in their own classrooms. Idiosyncratic mannerisms, movement patterns, and even illegible handwriting on the board can all be revealed in a video. Discussing one's own tape with the teacher candidate models a reflective teaching stance, in contrast to evaluation.

For teacher candidates to benefit from this experience, however, it may be important that their own initial videotapes be for teacher candidate eyes only. This is a tool for self-assessment, not evaluation by the mentor teacher, some other teacher, or a university supervisor. It is very helpful if the mentor teacher is not even in the room during the taping, and the camera is operated by a student.

If teacher candidates videotape a lesson at the beginning of the student teaching experience, during the middle, and at the end, they can reflect on their own growth and change as teachers. They will have an opportunity to see whether they "fixed" trouble spots that they identified in earlier lessons. As the teacher candidate and mentor teacher become comfortable in their relationship, the videotapes could be viewed and discussed if both agree to do so.

Examining Multiple Perspectives

Because teaching is a skill that grows and changes and teachers do things differently as their careers progress, it is really important that the teacher candidate does not feel compelled to emulate the mentor teacher completely. Furthermore, if a single mentor teacher is the only teacher with whom a teacher candidate works, this can give him or her a very narrow view of the profession and limited exposure to teaching practices. Mentor teachers should make it a point to recommend observations of teachers with very different teaching styles and diverse classrooms. Moreover, by observing other teachers, teacher candidates can get a broader picture of the school and how curriculums overlap.

In every high school department there are teachers who approach the same topic or lesson in different ways. This is a result of a variety of teaching styles and even transfers over to the planning phase of teaching. One teacher may know in October what will be on the final exam in January, while another may not know what she will be doing next week because she does not know what direction the students will take as they are given choices and options in their own learning. A teacher's approach may change dramatically across her teaching career or as a result of new students and contexts.

Patti is an example of a reflective teacher whose teaching practices have changed tremendously over the past 20 years. She takes the time to explain to her teacher candidates what research or observations have changed her practice. Again, this discussion about the evolution of teaching encourages the teacher candidate to adopt a reflective stance in which teaching approaches can change or develop as situations or students warrant those changes. This change does not mean, however, that the initial practice was wrong, but that given the students and the situation, a better way of approaching instruction might enhance student learning.

SUPPORTING PROFESSIONAL DEVELOPMENT

Reversing Roles in Conferencing

After teacher candidates complete an activity with a small group of students or present a portion or all of a lesson to an entire class, they need feedback from the mentor teacher. This is not always an easy task. As a new mentor teacher, Mindi was not prepared for the difficulty of responding to a teacher candidate's performance:

> Feedback seems like such an easy area. One difficulty we had was that Brian was really doing a good job, especially for a student teacher. No, he wasn't doing everything the way I would have done it, but he was trying different approaches and teaching styles and activities and having mixed success. So what do you say to that? I felt compelled to admire his willingness to try different things and to adjust as the classes went along. Also, the classes went well. Even the more difficult class he handled with as much success as I did. Learning how to compliment and then constructively criticize was more difficult than I expected it to be. I discovered I had to look for very specific things he did well and then look for specific things I thought could be changed to make classes run better or more smoothly or give the students a chance to learn more. I don't know if I ever really did this well; I wanted to pick larger issues and small, specific things. I wanted him to have issues to think about as a reflective practitioner and small things to change to show definite improvements.

Mindi's internal conflict is common with many mentor teachers. There is a delicate balance between nurturing and guidance and critique.

Following the example of peer coaching models, Beth initially asks the teacher candidate, "How do you feel about the lesson?" After allowing the teacher candidate time to respond, Beth then asks, "What did you like about the lesson?" And that question is followed by, "What would you do differently if you could teach it over?" Beth only listens to the responses of the teacher candidate and does not offer any of her observations or comments until the teacher candidate has answered all three questions. This gives the teacher candidate a sense of control over the conference and allows the teacher candidate time to reflect on the lesson, not on the comments or observations of the mentor teacher. Beth explains:

> I have found that anything I observe about a teacher candidate that I want to discuss and possibly pose as an area of improvement usually comes out in the postlesson conference from the teacher candidate, not from me. Then I am there to provide feedback that they ask for or that addresses a problem that they see. I do not ever want a teacher candidate to sit down after a lesson with an "Okay, what did I do wrong?" stance and sit while I do all the talking. Teaching is an art, and the artist has to have a sense of control over the growth process, or it can be a brutal situation for the teacher candidate.

This does not mean that the mentor teacher should not discuss weaknesses in a teacher candidate's performance. What is important is to provide the opportunity for teacher candidates to self-assess before being critiqued by the mentor teacher. Such an approach establishes trust between the two— an essential component if the teacher candidate is to grow and develop as an educator.

Saying the Hard Things

Even in the most ideal programs there are times when having a teacher candidate may put a mentor teacher in an awkward position. Problems may range from teacher candidates associating improperly with students to consistently arriving late or not preparing lesson plans. And there may be times when no matter how direct a mentor teacher is, the teacher candidate does not clearly understand the teacher's situation and does not accept her judgment. This is a difficult time to be a mentor teacher. All the relationship building stands in peril.

Each situation requires a personal touch from the mentor teacher, but we have found several methods consistently help us at these difficult times. The dialogue journal is the first place to begin (see Chapter 3). Here the situation can be objectified and analyzed. Eager for feedback, teacher candidates often write in their dialogue journals, "How am I doing?" The mentor teacher then has the opportunity to explain in writing why things like arrival time are important. Small problems, if allowed to accumulate, can easily become large ones.

If a problem persists, however, it can be helpful to enlist the support of the university advisor or another teacher, even if it is only to have a sounding board for what the mentor teacher wants to discuss with the teacher candidate (see Chapter 16). The university advisor, graduate assistant, or even assistant principal can facilitate communicating concerns to the teacher candidate. Creating an action plan that includes the problems discussed with the teacher candidate, the responsibilities of all involved, the expected outcomes, and a date and time for revisiting the issues is also a helpful approach to problem solving.

Regardless of the approach, the most important thing we have learned is that problems cannot be ignored. Mentor teachers have the dual responsibility of supporting a developing teacher candidate and ensuring that student learning in their classrooms is not hindered in any way (see Chapter 4). Early intervention and support help teacher candidates become stronger. Ignoring issues or postponing the hard business of dealing with them will not make them go away. Teacher candidates, we have found, are resilient for the most part and respect honesty from their mentor teachers when it is accompanied by visible support.

Letting Go

Christina found that one of the challenges of being a mentor teacher was stepping back and giving her teacher candidate room to explore and room to fail. She found that her overwhelming desire for everyone to have a positive experience was difficult to realize. "This year, letting go was especially hard . . . because I wanted Amy to have a positive experience. I just wanted everything to be okay for her. I wanted our students to accept her as they had accepted me."

After getting out of the classroom, and out of Amy's way, Christina found it hard not to intervene for her or to "fix" Amy's problems:

Probably the most difficult was accepting the fact that the teacher candidate will not have a wonderful day everyday. Why should she? No teachers do. As Amy shared her failures and fiascoes with me, I was an active listener, and I sympathized with her. However, I could not and should not try to fix things for her. She needed to find strategies for survival that would help her during her first year and the following years when I wouldn't be around.

This became especially difficult for Christina when students in her fourth-period class began to give Amy problems, refusing to do their work, saying cruel things under their breath, and finally playing a practical joke on Amy. Christina did intervene and talk to students away from class:

I yelled, threatened, and promised that my wrath would be upon them if they did not change their behavior. I worried all that weekend about how I could make them stop giving Amy a hard time. Finally, I realized that all my talking and pleading was not going to help. They were going to have to decide to accept her, and eventually they did. Several weeks later, they were her favorite class, responding expertly to class discussions and always showing her the same respect that they had shown me.

Christina learned that she could be supportive without intervening when problems occurred, and as a result Amy emerged a stronger teacher.

Staying Busy

Unfortunately many teachers in this profession like having a student teacher mainly for the break or the opportunity to relax a little. Although this can be a perk if you have a teacher candidate who is capable and effective, it can be a disastrous outlook if you end up with a teacher candidate who needs a great deal of guidance and attention. Mentor teachers who perceive that having a teacher candidate is going to give them some time off—when it often means *more* work—can easily communicate their frustration to the teacher candidate, making the situation even more uncomfortable. It is important for a mentor teacher to model professionalism when she is out of the classroom and the teacher candidate takes over.

Many mentor teachers utilize that time reading professional literature, planning a new unit from scratch, catching up on organizing files, or handling a big school-wide project, such as organizing a fund raiser or awards program. Others accept teacher researcher roles with their student teachers to collect and analyze data about shared questions. Beth is very conscious of how her teacher candidate sees her spending her time during the student teaching process. This comes from her own experience as a young teacher:

It was my second year of teaching, and I still needed the guidance and support that I [received] when I was a student teacher. It was the middle of the year, and my energy was lagging. At that time we had four student teachers in our department. I was sympathetic with their position because it [had been] so recently my own situation. One day, during a class, I went to the planning room to get copies of a handout I left on my desk. When I walked in, the lights were off, and the mentor teachers in my department were watching a newly released video in the planning room. I was confused by what I saw as a lack of consideration for the student teachers as well as the other teachers in the trenches at that moment. And when I returned to my room, it was with the attitude of a child who had been punished and had to go to work.

Beth understands that particular situation more clearly from her present perspective as a mentor. Without the presence of teacher candidates in classrooms, teachers would not have the time to preview videotapes during the school day, which was indeed what this group had been doing. In this instance, they were not neglecting their duties or abusing their authority. Nonetheless, Beth appreciates how those perceptions might be entertained by department colleagues without teacher candidates and even by teacher candidates themselves if mentor teachers are not explicit about their professional development goals while teacher candidates are in charge of the mentor teachers' classrooms.

CONCLUSION

Our collaborative inquiry community provides a supportive network for mentors to pose and resolve problems emerging from relationships with individual teacher candidates. Looking carefully at patterns of tensions common to many relationships over time has helped the group to acknowledge and honor the teacher candidate's perspective as well as the mentor teacher's.

The sustained dialogue about mentoring has helped teachers to conceptualize the mentor teacher/teacher candidate relationship as one characterized by unequal power, status, and authority. A teacher candidate watches everything a mentor teacher does. All the watching is not without judgment; this is to be expected. However, when mentors take time to build rapport and look at their teacher candidates as partners, the teacher candidates become participants with personal investment in students and the classroom beyond what is expected from mere "visitors" who arrive to teach for a few weeks. When the relationship works, mentors not only contribute to the development of young, effective professionals, but simultaneously become agents of their own ongoing learning about teaching.

CHAPTER 3

The Dialogue Journal

Jerelyn Wallace

Jerelyn Wallace discovered that a dialogue journal added a special dimension to collaboration with her teacher candidate, Erin McDermott. Through observations, questions, and reflections, they—along with Peg and Sally on campus— explored the rich, problematic, and exciting insights of shared teaching. In this piece, Jerelyn has selected excerpts from their extensive e-mail journals to give readers the flavor of what is possible when partners agree to engage in conversation more meaningful, different, and beyond the rush of daily talk.

I suppose that most people who find their way into English education have already discovered the power of keeping a personal journal. Certainly that power has been revealed to me many times over, as in my life I've discovered through journaling a safe place to explore my thoughts and feelings, without distraction. In my journal I dream big. I cry there too, with uncharacteristic abandon. A journal is a place of poetry, words, and sketches, capturing (however cryptically) the impressions of the life it catalogues. The expression itself is powerful, but amazing things start to happen when journaling becomes an instrument for reflection. Examining your recorded images, you begin to see the cycles of events in your life. You see honest patterns and begin to recognize the appropriate process for desired change. This reflective process has been very meaningful in my personal life.

An English teacher for 9 years, I've also known the power of communicating with my students through in-class journal assignments and projects. In that space I've shared great joys and sorrows that might have never been revealed to me otherwise. In the distance and silence of written words, students say what they think, and beyond the distractions inherent in the classroom, I hear them. The journal is a useful tool in trying to make sense of the persons we teach, and a powerful conduit through which we may respond candidly to their lives and views.

And as I've learned working within our collaborative community, the back and forth of journal writing and response is also a powerful tool for professional edification and communication among mentor teachers, teacher candidates, and university faculty. The *dialogue journal* (or DJ) was a new concept to me when I began my work with the collaborative inquiry community 3 years ago, but I was immediately intrigued by the notion, which appealed to my love of both expression *and* office supplies. Distributing a stack of beautiful "blank books," our university colleagues challenged each of the mentor teachers to begin a written dialogue with his or her teacher candidate, a forum for observations, questions, and reflections that would chronicle the year's teaching practice as well as the evolving relationship between mentor teacher and teacher candidate. Periodically, the university folks would jump into the conversation, adding their own responses.

Over the years, my colleagues in the program and I have embraced this "assignment" with varying degrees of enthusiasm and success. On the one hand, some mentors and teacher candidates spend so much time talking, that the dialogue journal seems a redundant effort. And considering the rigorous schedule and demanding paper load of both teachers and teacher candidates, it's no wonder that time and energy for this kind of professional writing are elusive. But on the other hand, some mentors and teacher candidates have used the dialogue journal as a *tool*. The exchange may take on a life of its own, become a welcomed place to record the joys and frustrations of teaching practice, and provide a forum through which communication among teacher candidates, mentors, and university colleagues is greatly enriched. Additionally, the dialogue journal itself, as a *reflective* instrument, in both the long and short term, gives incredible insight into the process of the year— the progress of students, personal growth as an educator, the evolution of relationships and connections all the way around.

Personally, I've been in both camps. But my second year in our group, I did share a dialogue journal that I'll never forget with an unforgettable teacher candidate, Erin McDermott, and two university colleagues, Peg Graham and Sally Ross. Erin and I "clicked" from the beginning, sharing a similar educational philosophy and life view. The DJ (significantly, kept via e-mail) became a part of our routine, an (almost) immediate, unobtrusive, and deeply revealing instrument. It greatly enhanced the shared relationships and simplified the many tasks before us. Alone at my computer, usually late at night, I was able to bypass the many distractions of the school day to give my undivided attention to a particular issue or an immediate need. Or sometimes, we just talked. It was great fun and a very productive use of time.

While by no means inclusive, I hope the following excerpts from our journal will illustrate the different *kinds* of thinking that the DJ encourages as well as the blending of voices and perspectives that can take place when everyone participates.

OBSERVATIONS

Erin: Today's writing: images of fall. As I walked around the room, I noticed that John and Ann did jot lists without being prompted. I was so excited. Then Lucy was stuck for a topic, and I suggested a jot list to her, and she seemed to like the idea. I guess it worked, because the next time I checked, she was writing away like a madwoman. I thought that was really cool. Something I noticed—the class becomes almost 100% on task when you move through the room when they are writing.

Erin: Brian, what to think? When I observed him today, it seemed like he was just staring at his book, not really following along while we went through "The Prologue." But then he answered the question about The Reeve, so I knew that he was with us in *some* capacity. I just don't know. This is going to sound awful, but sometimes, I forget that he is in class. I mean, he is so quiet and nondescript that I sometimes just pass over him when I look around the room. I find that it's sometimes hard for me to "see" the quiet kids in class. I am trying to make a conscious effort to correct this when I teach. I know I should be sent to teacher purgatory for admitting it, but it's true. Do you have any thoughts?

Jerelyn: As far as feeling guilty for not noticing every detail of every kid—well, don't obsess about it. Interest in and love of people is a gift you possess and want to share. As long as you maintain that base, you'll know how to direct your energy. Wasn't it Helen Keller who said, "I can't do everything, but I can do something." That's the attitude to have.

Erin: I like the way you start every class with a "Good morning class . . ." I think it really brings the kids together, which is where you want them to be as soon as possible. I know that you recommended that I do this during my lesson on ballads, and I just forgot. But I will make it a point to do it from now on.

Erin: Jacob—man, he lost it yesterday. I really felt bad for you, because you were in a situation where you simply *had* to be firm with him. I think you came to a good compromise though ("Let's continue this debate after school."). That was the first time that I glimpsed that side of him, and I have to admit that it was really scary.

Peg: I'm always glad to hear when teacher candidates have seen their mentor teachers handle a situation of discipline adroitly. You'll know to anticipate what Jacob (and others like Jacob) can reveal about themselves unexpectedly. Although teachers are expected to behave consistently, students have trigger points that unveil different, unpredictable aspects of their character. Like a boy scout, you learn to "be prepared." Cases like Jacob will help you to imagine some of the possibilities associated with student behavior.

QUESTIONS

Erin: I wanted to let Peg and Sally in on our discussion about Steve. This is a student from our eleventh-grade class. I think Greg [another teacher] put it best when he said, "Steve Jones taught me patience." He teaches *me* every time I see him. Anyway, I shadowed him through all of his classes one day for the language project [see Chapter 6], and at one point, he introduced me as his mom. I didn't think anything about it until the following week when he started saying, "Hey mom!" in the hall and started telling everyone around him, "Hey, that's my mom." In class, he asks questions like, "What time is dinner?" and says things like, "Would you tell John to leave me alone?" I thought he was just being weird, but then I talked to another teacher who told me his mother is not in his life and that he lives with his uncle. Now, I don't really think that he sees me as a mother figure (but it was weird, of all the things to call me . . .), and it doesn't really *bother* me. Should I just let it go, unless it becomes disruptive?

Peg: I've got to admit, Steve sounds like he's seeking attention, and *maybe* he's doing it in a way that also registers a need for a mother figure. On the other hand, I'd be uncomfortable with a student who carries that into the classroom. I think it probably could become a disruptive influence, but I'm not there to see it, so I could be off the mark. If, as Greg says, Steve is one of those kids who knows how to try a teacher's patience, he may be a master button pusher. If it makes you or Jerelyn or the kids in your classroom uncomfortable, I'd talk to him individually about it. He may find it sufficient to know you're mildly flattered by the title but it's just not appropriate given the classroom context. Would he understand that and be willing to cooperate? Or would that add fuel to his niggling ways?

Sally: Steve who teaches patience. That was my Amy [a student of mine]. "Mom" is a *kind* thing to be called. He needs attention, I'd guess. Here's a new way. It'll get old. Read nothing more into it, Erin.

Jerelyn: About Steve: I agree with Peg's and Sally's comments. I think it's just Steve showing off, but personally, I'd stop it. An upbeat, private chat: "This is kind of weird to me and I wish you wouldn't do it," would put an end to "Mommy Erin," I think.

Erin: Eleventh grade—Paul. What do I do about his swearing in Spanish? Now I know that I left myself wide open by admitting that I know Spanish. (It seemed like a harmless question, but now I realize that there are no harmless questions!) I know that many of the kids in class didn't understand what he said, and I didn't want to draw attention to him by getting mean or uptight. But then again, saying things like, "C'mon," "All right now," or "Don't go there," just doesn't seem adequate. Do you have any suggestions?

Jerelyn: About Paul swearing in Spanish: It should not be tolerated any more than swearing in English would be tolerated. A firm, no-nonsense correction is in order. Say, "This is not acceptable behavior. If you use that kind of language in the classroom, I will deal with it as though you had spoken the words in English." I wouldn't bring it up in retrospect, but if it ever happens again (count on it), act.

Erin: I have a question that has been bothering me for a while: What do you do with a kid who just simply *does not care?* In the eleventh-grade class, there are a few kids (Jacob, John) who seem resigned to the "fact" that they are going to fail. For example, Jacob made 20% on his vocabulary quiz. I know that it isn't a mental deficiency, so what's the problem??!! And kids who don't turn their homework in consistently—what do you do? If the kid thinks he is going to fail anyway, then it doesn't help to remind him of how much that missing homework will hurt his grade. I realize that some kids will fail, but it's hard to see it happen right before your eyes. At what point do you get the parents involved?

Peg: Big question here. We can't force kids to be motivated and engaged, but we can do all we can to find out what influences are working on these students. Maybe your research question is right in front of you. What about a couple of case studies? Sometimes parents can help, but an apathetic student usually completely understands the consequences of his/her actions.

Jerelyn: I wish I knew the answer to *that* question. My approach has been everything from warm and fuzzy ("You'll *feel* so much better if I'm not on your back all the time!") to public sanction in class ("What do you mean you're quitting!!)," or the old favorite . . . "Do you really *want* to repeat this course?!" You do what you can to encourage and provide opportunities for success, try always to maintain a positive class climate, and remember that ultimately, it's their *choice.*

Peg: I'm intrigued by your discussion of switching from "Johnny Bear" to "The Lottery" because even some of the folks in our class had trouble "getting it." What does that mean to you exactly? I always found my students liked "Bear" precisely because it was a challenge. We spent time looking at the end from the perspective of character motivation. As they struggled to put together their own responses to the characters' actions and the information provided by the text, it became a classic example of Rosenblatt's reader response theory of "not any, but many" interpretations being supported by the text. I don't know your students, though, so all of this discussion may be moot as far as you're concerned. It is a difficult story, but there are a number of ways to pique student interest. How it's presented and how you support/ structure their reading experiences with it would be key.

Erin: Well Peg, you've made me reconsider "Johnny Bear" again. You see, I *really* liked the story, but I was afraid that if *our* class struggled with it, then my class of (some very) average eleventh graders would be lost. But I think you're right. The story is open for interpretations—I just wonder if they would. Jerelyn, what do you think?

Jerelyn: Go with "Johnny Bear" if that's what you want to do. So what if they don't all "get it." Get what? They'll all get *something.*

Erin: Additionally, another teacher suggested that I put marks in the grade book next to the names of students who were either really good or really bad during discussion. Since there are only a few per day, this probably wouldn't take too long. I also thought of another idea [based on her teacher research]. I thought that, at the beginning of next quarter, I would sit down with the classes and brainstorm a list of appropriate behaviors and consequences for behaving inappropriately. Then I would type this up as a list of class rules, and have each student and their parents sign it. I could then say, "Hey, you were aware of the rules and chose to disregard them, knowing full well what the punishment would be." What do you think?

Jerelyn: About taking grades for individual participation in discussion, etc.: I'm afraid this kind of method would be overwhelming and would (no doubt) reduce *me* to a quivering mass of exposed nerves. You're trying to "give credit" for each aspect of a student's performance. If you want to try it, go for it, but be sure you've thought about the best use of time. I've been satisfied that students under my grading scheme "get what they deserve," and I don't drive myself crazy trying to categorize something like discussion.

About brainstorming class rules and sending something home: I'm not sure how I feel about that. It's a great thing to do if you anticipate a problem (beginning of the year—new teacher) or are having problems, neither of which really apply to our situation. First, third, and fifth [period classes] work so beautifully (and I don't foresee a great change when you take over)—and fourth period—well, we're at critical mass. As I've said, the next time someone screws up in there, I'm coming down hard, on individuals, not on the whole class. So, in short, if it ain't broken, don't fix it. I've found that if you walk in expecting proper conduct, that's (mostly) what you'll get. Then your discipline strategies become matters of individual correction and attention. That's better and more productive.

Erin: The daily grades thing: I think I haven't really been clear with you on it. I think you have an idea of something that would be a lot more involved than what I had in mind. I wanted to keep a daily record of class participation, but I didn't want anything that was going to be too burdensome. I was just going to write down everyone's name on a sheet of paper. Then, after class, instead of putting a grade by everyone's name (eke!), I would just put pluses or minuses next to those who deserved them, and as you know, there would only be a couple of them in each class. Then I would give a weekly grade, based on how they did during the week. I don't think it is as time-consuming as it sounds. Believe me, the last thing that I want is to take up more time!

The rules thing: A lot of the kids said that they liked to have an established set of class rules, and if I have a list, with the accompanying consequences, I think it makes things clear to everyone. They know if they are breaking a rule, and what it is going to cost them if they do.

There isn't any confusion. Also, it covers me, in case a student or parent says, "I think this punishment is unfair." I think that when I come in the spring, it's another opportunity for me to establish my authority, because I'm not the "guest" teacher anymore. It's kind of hard for me now, because, even when I am teaching, I don't feel like it's *my* class. But in the spring, I think that will change. I will feel a little more permanent. Now, they know that they aren't going to see me the next day. But they will have to see me everyday in the spring. I think that it would help me establish myself as the lead teacher.

Peg: The bookkeeping aspect of the daily participation grade can be a nightmare. It's a matter of getting into really good habits of observation and recording. I've always considered myself better at the former than the latter. Throughout my teaching career, we were required to be in the hall between classes, which sometimes made it difficult to record impressions of one group before the next one came in. I suggest you experiment some and see what kinds of record keeping seem most natural for your organizational preferences. You may be able to use a combination of assessments—provided by your observations as well as students' records of their own participation. Maybe if you all get into the habit of taking 3 minutes at the end of class to jot down the nature and degree of participation, you might have a much more powerful assessment of what actually unfolds. Just more food for thought on the issue at hand.

Erin: Rough day today—feeling overwhelmed by the material to teach in the spring. Six units just seem like a lot, but I know I can do it. I just have to figure out how! I was feeling pretty low, and Susanna [another teacher candidate] explained that it is like when a huge paper is assigned. You don't know what to do or where to start, but it eventually works itself out. I guess my plans will too.

Peg: Erin, you're making noises like a teacher here. As I read your words, I'm reflecting on how we used to throw teacher candidates to the wolves by making them adjust to school, students, mentor teachers—all while they were trying to plan. I know it feels overwhelming, but you're going to have lots of support and planning will get easier. It's time-consuming, yes, but doable. Be sure to talk to Sally and Jerelyn and me when you find yourself paralyzed by these demands. We can help. We've experienced all of this. It goes with the territory.

Sally: I want you to print out that message and if you choose to teach one day to reread it about October when you would give anything for the luxury of 2 months to plan six units! Ask Jerelyn about her first year! Enjoy—you will! [In class this week] we'll ask you to develop a timeline to show yourself how you can accomplish all of this. We'll also brainstorm good first-week activities—raid files, go back to the *English Journal* for ideas, see books, manuals, etc., talk to everyone you can, and, of course, read all the materials. So, you're right on track for now—you just don't believe it yet!

Jerelyn: Don't worry about the six units. We all know you're working hard. Keep it up, keep balanced, and don't sweat it—it *will* all come together!

REFLECTIONS

Erin: While you were gone, Mr. Smith came in to give a PSAT lecture to the eleventh graders. He was so discouraging, basically telling the kids that their only option was either cosmetology or technical school. I was so mad! I try so hard to convince these kids that they really do have potential, and then he comes in and basically tells them that they don't have much to look forward to. Now, I realize that these kids probably will not continue on to college, but it doesn't help to be reminded of this fact!

Jerelyn: I think it depends on your approach. Suggesting technical school (or whatever) as a second-class alternative to college is terrible for students' self-esteem and doesn't reflect prospects for success either. (Hired a plumber lately?) It's important for us to be as excited about vocational choices as college choices.

Peg: Jerelyn's *right* on the money!

Erin: Of course, I really hate being a [mean person], but sometimes there's just no way around it!

Sally: I decided it was like being a parent—a kind disciplinarian— though it felt [mean] to me at first. You and I were "good kids"—we don't know what the voice of censure sounds like so it all sounds mean to us. Take on the role of the parent who cares—just let them know the parameters, no apologies needed. You are helping them when you do so! No matter *what* they say!

Jerelyn: Yesterday, I read Kurt and Rick's A+ papers to the class, which was *a big time* ego boost for both of these silent and sullen boys.

In his essay, Rick told of his grandmother's straightforward methods of discipline, and how she had said once when he asked permission to go out on a date, "If you can't do yo' class work, you can't do no man's work, if you know what I mean." Understanding, the class erupted in laughter, and Rick suddenly interjected, "That's a *direct quote.*" Big fun. And Kurt's essay gives some insight into his current demeanor. His grandfather (they were very close) had a stroke and is now living with the family, not communicating much. Real sad and hard to take.

Erin: Rick is so quiet in class, but such an amazing writer. I'm having second thoughts about his exam. Yes, he did base his essay on the idea that Beowulf was a hero, a *stupid* hero, but a hero nonetheless. Rick did support his argument—supported it *well,* in fact. He was simply offering *his* interpretation of the text. Just because it wasn't my interpretation, does that mean it's wrong? I don't think so!

Erin: Yesterday went off without a hitch. Each period displayed their own personalities to the nth degree. First period was ultra-quiet; third period was absolutely angelic; and fourth period was . . . well . . . it was fourth period. (It is physically impossible to talk and read at the same time. I've tried it. It doesn't work. Alas, they didn't believe me!) Fifth period was typical too. I think Glen really got into the Thoreau stuff. He seemed really involved during the tape. It was the same way with Lucy. They both seemed really interested in the tape and what I had to say about "Where I Lived and What I Lived For." I think it would be cool if they were turned onto Thoreau. He is an absolute favorite of mine; the man changed my life! Interestingly the parts of the tape that most people remembered were the excerpts from "Civil Disobedience"—the entire back corner was paraphrasing it. I think that this would be an interesting reading for them, but I'm almost afraid to give these kids any fuel for revolution!

Peg: Ah—and there's the rub! If you were to really get your kids to love Thoreau as much as you do, you'd probably have to go with their interest in "Civil Disobedience." And that might establish an atmosphere of revolution that you'd find . . . what? Intimidating? Upsetting to the status quo? We want our kids to use their literacy in ways that empower them, and we want them to gain a measure of control over their own lives, *but* we don't want them to begin that in our classrooms or our schools. It sets up an interesting dilemma, doesn't it?

Erin: What a day! I'm glad I took a little space to reflect, because the good things really outweighed the bad. Things like . . . Larry reading the poem to an absolutely silent class. (They were wonderful for him.) Also, Max gave some really cool answers to my questions. Oh, and silent Timothy actually offered an interpretation too—I was so excited! So, I'm glad I found some good things to remember.

Sally: Always find the good in the day too! Bravo! It's so easy to let the bad overwhelm you (or the perceived bad). I even started a separate book when I was [teaching] at Cedar Shoals called "The Good Book" in which I made myself write down each day what I did well or what went well. I lived for that book many a day! So glad you can do that, Erin!

Peg: What a wonderful turn you make here. You frontload the day's description with the bad outweighing the good and then remember to point out everything you *can* feel good about. What a gift. It's easy to focus too hard on what's wrong, less easy to uncover the good when that feeling envelopes you. Good for you. Pull it up to serve you whenever you can.

Jerelyn: It's amazing how much power you have when you establish a kind and cheerful rapport with students. With such a base, just the sideways "teacher look" and a firm *"excuse me"* is quickly followed by a sincere apology in the hall—bravo Erin!

Jerelyn: Erin, I too feel we were moving parallel but not connecting yesterday, and that's a new energy for us. But it's all good, even these downward spirals. Always know even cycles of decline move along and then it's up, up, and up to a more relaxed and gratifying time. So, that's what I'm telling *myself.* After the birth of the year (such beauty, this one!), we're cycling into the routine of the task at hand. A year is long and a year has cycles. Each class and each person in it has cycles. And so do we. It's just learning to pace ourselves accordingly and trying to stay happy in the process. That's life, I suppose.

Erin: I feel the same way about cycles. On the way home from school today, I was thinking about all of the different cycles and planes that I am passing through right now. It's amazing. One moment, it seems life is moving so slowly, and then I blink, and a month is gone. I find myself changing, realizing and accepting who I am, and feeling good about it. I realize that I don't have to explain or justify myself. I am who I am.

After many years of working with student teachers, one thing seems clear: the success of the mentor teacher/teacher candidate relationship hinges on both parties truly understanding the perspective of the other, and on a willingness to honestly evaluate cause and effect in the classroom and beyond. Precise and reflective communication, therefore, is essential to give the experience the best chance for real success. The resonance of the dialogue journal *supplements* what is achieved by verbal discussion, and the reflective process inherent in journaling encourages everyone to formulate clearly and apply their philosophical approaches to the questions of teaching practice. Mentor teacher/teacher candidate pairs who willingly incorporate the dialogue journal into their routines, who personalize the instrument and make it work, will find the results well worth the time and energy. This is a good thing, for ourselves, and especially for our students who benefit from our careful self-reflection.

CHAPTER 4

Giving Up My Kids: Two Mentor Teachers' Stories

Ellen Cowne & Susan Little

Ellen and Susan's voices will resonate for many mentor teachers who experience the pangs of sharing the students they love with a teacher candidate. Ellen acknowledges the range of conflicting emotions she had when she had to pass on her kids to John after 5 years of being their English teacher and during the last quarter she would be at this school. Susan, in a deeply honest voice, explores issues of responsibility and the mentor teacher's self-image. Teacher candidate and university readers will gain new insights into the very real tensions that surround a teacher's decision to share her students so that a newcomer can learn.

ELLEN'S STORY

For many teachers, behaving like a "human doing" is much easier than behaving like a "human being." Thus, it is more comfortable for teachers to begin doing something new than to stop doing something old—like working with the students who have consumed their time for the past 8 months. In my case, however, it was not just 7 or 8 months. I had been this group's English teacher in the ninth, tenth, eleventh, and twelfth grades and had pulled them from their eighth-grade English teacher once a week for gifted work. So 5 years had made us a class, a team, a family, a closely cemented group. They needed outside input because of their not having another English teacher, and I had done what I could to provide this by having *many* outside speakers and visiting lecturers. John, my teacher candidate, had been with us all year as an engaging class member and "guest" teacher. However, if the truth were known, I really did not want to share this class with anyone, not even John. They were mine, and I was invested in their lives—their studies, their college plans, their romances, their cliques.

Yet when John's turn came to work with them full time in the spring, I needed to let them go. This feeling of "giving them away" was not uncommon to me since I had worked with student teachers before, but this year was different, not only because John had been there all year, but also because I would be leaving my position in June to go to another school. I would miss these students, and I did not want to let them go. But John deserved his chance with them. This was his time to learn, and their opportunity to learn from him. I faced a time of many emotions.

The first emotion I felt was jealousy. These students really liked John. They told me how much he knew and how "cool" he was. He had stood in line on campus to get concert tickets for some of them and had immediately sealed his place in their hearts. They began to write notes on the board to him with messages such as, "We love you, Mr. Parr." Those were the things they used to say to *me,* and I was bothered. But like a mother who must give her son to his first girl friend, I was also glad that his experience was positive. If I had to send them off into the world of other teachers, I was glad it was to someone with whom they could relate.

The second emotion I had was a rigid adherence to "my" type of teaching. I was positive that since they had done things my way for so many years, it would be an imposition to ask them to change. Wrong again!! His method was much more workshop directed. I had never been able to make this work, so my excuse had been that the students simply did not work well with that method. John showed me that they did fine this way—his way—and they liked it. He sat at a desk and talked with them instead of to them. I was sure that the discipline would suffer if he was not walking around in a monitoring posture. But it didn't. He had them sit in a circle on the floor and discuss their research proposals instead of requiring a written proposal as I had done. They did not get off task, as I was sure that they would. He required them to come up with five questions to ask him each day instead of his coming up with questions to ask them. And they grew. And he grew. And I finally grew, too. I had learned that to bend was not to break.

Another strong desire for me was to stay in class—just in case he needed me, or they needed me. Why should I leave the room when I simply could retreat to a corner and work on my computer and senior class sponsor responsibilities? But Jiminy Cricket with his ever still, small voice reminded me that just as I would not be a welcome guest on my teenager's dates, I was extra baggage in his classroom. The revelation finally had hit. It was "his" classroom. I must take my work to another station as often as possible and let him sink or swim. I would like to say I was afraid he would sink; however, I wonder if I was not afraid he might swim and do so smoothly, thus proving the students did not need me at all.

The most important emotion I felt, however, was the calm that overcame me when I finally let go. I realized I didn't have to stop being a teacher. Instead I could become a teacher-observer, a teacher of teachers, a learner myself, and a giver. So I could continue in my addiction of being a human doing; my doings simply would be different ones. I began to leave the classroom more, both during class and during the time before school and after school when the students would come in to socialize. If they wanted to tell me about a wonderful poem they had written, they told him. When I remained in the room during class, I listened to his responses in order to give him feedback on how many girls as opposed to boys he was calling on, how much wait time he was giving them, and how quickly he began class after the bell rang. I found that I actually did have suggestions to offer that would help him become more efficient. At one point, the students began to ask rapid-fire questions, pretending a confusion they really did not feel and causing a confusion that they intended. Finally!! Here was a way I could help. I suggested to John that should they try this again, he might try telling them to write down all their questions, collecting them, and addressing them one at a time. Many times, I knew as an experienced teacher, students ask questions to test a teacher's patience instead of his knowledge. As I began to feel less threatened, I began to enjoy watching my students enjoy John and to appreciate that he liked the students as much as I did. I felt like a matchmaker—an important person again!

I had always thought that the most important thing I could give to my students was myself. Now I knew the most important thing I could do for them was to give them someone else. The best gift to John was to give happy students to him and to relish their relationship and my part in it. For mine was a big part. No young teacher candidate can succeed if the teacher does not give up her hold. The mentor teacher must take the risk and trust in the teacher candidate's abilities. W. B. Yeats, in "The Second Coming," said, "Things fall apart / The center cannot hold." True in many worlds and times. But in the world of teacher candidates, supervising teachers, students, and emotions, things fall apart if the teacher does not let go. The center, teaching and learning, stays intact. The risk is great, but the outcome is worth the chance taken when a mentor teacher learns to give her students away.

SUSAN'S STORY

Every year I consider working with a teacher candidate, I have to confront troublesome concerns in the back of my mind. Some of these worries come from a sense of responsibility toward my students; others stem from an ongoing process of self-evaluation and my own self-image in my classroom, school, and community. These factors can create enough anxiety to make the entire mentoring relationship a negative one. I suspect these same concerns keep other teachers from ever becoming mentors. But then I think of the powerful reasons and ways that mentoring enhances not only my work but also the profession. A year-long program helps me work through my worries as well as the individual needs of each teacher candidate and group of students. As mentor teachers, we need to let our teacher candidates understand the struggles *we* go through each year in making the decision to accept them into our world.

Responsibility

The first difficulty for me is giving up my students to a "practice" teacher, as we used to call them. Allowing a teacher candidate to "practice" on my students suggests that the students are being shortchanged. Of course, we all need to practice and learn from trial and error (see Chapter 12), but do the same students deserve this experimental approach every year? Because I live in a university town, my students have had many teacher candidates across the years. I have serious concerns and even some guilt about asking students to have a student teacher instead of a "real" teacher hired by, evaluated by, and obligated to the school system and community. All I need to hear is one or two young people complain, and my complex that they need to have a "real" teacher quickly surfaces.

Along these same lines, I wonder, "Will the teacher candidate really take care of my students?" I take my responsibility as teacher seriously, spending much time and energy to develop rapport with classes and individual students. The result is something akin to the parent–child relationship, in which I see myself as instructor, encourager, and disciplinarian. Like it or not, every teacher candidate is *not* cut out to be a teacher. All of us have heard, and many of us have experienced, horror stories of student teachers who were indeed unacceptable in their interactions with adolescents. The agreement to invite a stranger into my classroom is almost as difficult as inviting a long-term guest to live in my home. Placing students in the hands of a teacher candidate asks me to depend on someone else to nurture my children.

Coupled with these issues is the concern about time. There is never enough time to accomplish all I think I need to do with my classes, and the fear of sacrificing several weeks to someone else's teaching sometimes makes me want to cut short the teacher candidate's interaction with classes. A recent student teacher, Jenny, was eager to take over classes from day one. I found myself trying to get in just one more unit before I yielded my juniors to her. I believe in what I teach; if I didn't, I wouldn't be a good mentor. But the push–pull of happily modeling for a teacher candidate, then having to walk off the stage can be traumatic.

All of these concerns emanate from a sense of responsibility toward my students. Mentoring teacher candidates has forced me to look at these problems. I have found that if I am honest with myself about my feelings and if I work with the student teacher instead of against him or her, I can deal with these issues easily. All of us were once beginning teachers as college students and on our first jobs. We were not the teachers then that we are now. Without the guidance of some able veteran, most of us would not have made it in the teaching profession. Experience has taught us that no student's education will be permanently ruined because of having sat through a few weeks with a less than exemplary teacher candidate. In fact, each new teacher often brings an approach or attitude to the classroom that can re-energize a class that has fallen into too much routine. So, the practice, nurturing, and time issues are not as major as they seem.

Another problem, although serious, does not have to be a disaster. "Is this student teacher prepared to teach?" I must ask every year. Not only may the teacher candidate not come prepared to teach a specific lesson (it happens more than we like to admit), but he or she may not be thoroughly grounded in the subject matter itself. People come into teaching from various points in their own educations, and some simply have not delved deeply enough into their specific subjects to lead a classroom discussion or follow students' questions. In addition, teacher candidates may have been narrow in their course selections and find themselves teaching material to which they have had little exposure. One student teacher came to my classes armed with Chaucer and Dickens; unfortunately, my students were studying American literature, which the young man had hardly seen since high school. That he would take an American literature course the following summer didn't help us now. Still others—as in any profession—have gotten by with minimal effort and as a result have little knowledge to draw upon and no work habits to aid them in catching up. Others have never worked with high school students or people from cultures other than their own; they are unprepared for the realities of American public schools today. Just thinking about turning a class over to an unprepared teacher candidate causes alarm for me and other mentor teachers.

I have found that if I help and supervise appropriately, we—the teacher candidate and mentor teacher—usually can manage. We can choose material that will allow the student teacher to learn on the job while still being sure that high school students are learning what they need. One teacher candidate who came my way several years ago had business-like and distinct enunciation but poor command of subject–verb agreement, a potentially embarrassing problem especially for an English teacher. She also knew little about the nineteenth-century literature we needed to teach. I steered her toward a review unit on verbs, and then a short poetry and composition unit. I asked her to write out everything she planned to say and do so that I could help her find grammatical errors and clear up possible trouble spots where she was uncertain in her knowledge. Although she began the year with difficulty, this teacher candidate worked hard to improve. She made mistakes, but she learned from them. Had we been limited to the typical 9 weeks of student teaching, I don't think she would have been so successful. Because I could truly mentor her as she readied herself for teaching, her progress was dramatic.

Self-Evaluation and Image

Beyond the issues related to my responsibilities to my students are my very honest personal concerns that get at the very core of who I am as teacher. I am one of those teachers who continuously evaluates myself. I frequently see aspects of my teaching that I could have done "better." Such honesty with myself and the uncertainty it engenders can be stressful. Adding to the situation a teacher candidate who may judge my work, can become threatening (see Chapter 5). All of the mentor teacher's "what ifs" emerge to shake my security.

What if the students like the student teacher better than they do me? This is an unspoken but always present question. Teacher candidates are so often more energetic than we veterans are, and certainly more idealistic. They bring youth to the classroom; they come armed with fun activities. I know that having students *like* me is not my primary goal, but the human need to be liked, to be appreciated, is just as real for me as it is for anybody else. Like Ellen above, I can easily fall into this worry trap.

What if the student teacher is better than I am? Perhaps this rarely admitted fear is at the bottom of many of the other reasons we give for not wanting to work with student teachers. Several teacher candidates I have mentored were unusually good teachers. My eager teacher candidate, Jenny, devised wonderful projects, allowed students to discuss their own ideas, and created small group tasks that were exciting. Jenny was energetic, knowledgeable, and innovative. My juniors loved her. As I observed her interaction with my classes, I did feel a little threatened. I wondered if the students would rather I did not come back. I questioned my own methods (see Chapter 5). Such discomfort quickly can make a mentor teacher decide not to enter into a similar situation again.

In truth, feeling somewhat threatened by youth and freshness is not entirely bad. Being made uncomfortable motivated me to examine thoroughly just what I was doing in the classroom on a day-to-day basis. Such self-examination has led me to incorporate some new approaches and to remove several worn-out, ineffective units. I found my passion for teaching rekindled and my energy increased as I planned anew.

What if the teacher candidate loses control? I need control to maintain my own personal comfort level in the classroom. Each of us thinks of control in terms of student behavior, student productivity, learning goals, and expectations that reflect the norms of our community. As the teacher candidate changes these parameters, we begin to worry. Mentor teachers are motivated somewhat by the awareness that administrators, parents, and students expect the teacher to shoulder the blame ultimately if students do not progress as they should. Giving up control of one's class is therefore linked to giving up control of one's own reputation and self-image, which have taken years to build.

When all is said and done, the anxieties that arise when we consider giving up our students to teacher candidates are real in that they can inhibit our effectiveness both as teachers and as mentors. As with other anxieties and concerns, they can be dealt with positively and turned into gains both for our students and for teacher candidates. One of the advantages of mentoring a teacher candidate throughout the year rather than supervising him or her for a quarter or a semester is that many of our fears and concerns are identified, discussed openly, and answered long before the teacher candidate begins extended teaching throughout the school day.

Teacher candidates need strong teaching experiences. The year-long program provides teacher candidates with an unprecedented opportunity to become effective teachers who enter the work force ready to do the job. We mentor teachers need practice, too—practice in being mentors who encourage and help develop those who will one day make our profession their own. I am convinced that some of the best teaching I do is the mentoring of teacher candidates. I am also convinced that some of the most important learning I personally have acquired recently has been from teacher candidates who shared themselves with me. The key is being open and honest about our own concerns and focusing our worries on the students we share.

CHAPTER 5

Growing from a Teacher Candidate Challenge: A Teacher Researcher Stance in Response to Tension

Chandra Adkins

When her teacher candidate held very different beliefs about pedagogy, Chandra Adkins began to examine more closely her own practice and the choices she made for her students. In this chapter, she discusses the process that led her to examine her practice, the teacher research that she conducted to help her think about her choices, and the productive results that emerged.

Having another adult in my classroom is always an exciting prospect for me. I enjoy being observed, like being videotaped, and am enough of a ham to love administrative evaluations. Having a teacher candidate is an enriching experience, and I have always valued the ways in which I, as a teacher, can learn from the teacher candidate. Teacher candidates bring in new ideas, new strategies for engaging students in material; they also ask hard questions about what I do and why I do it. Such questioning leads to an introspection one might not always gain from self-reflection. Try as they might, teachers don't always catch up on the newest readings and theories, and teacher candidates bring with them their awareness of texts, articles, and philosophy that they share with their mentor teachers.

I have been fortunate in my relationships with teacher candidates and practicum students with whom I've worked over the years. Teacher candidates who've shared my classroom in the past have all had philosophies similar to mine, and I've been able to remain pretty confident and assured of my status as teacher. However, for many mentor teachers and teacher candidates, the situation in a mentor teacher/student teaching relationship is not always as productive and positive as the ones to which I had become accustomed. In many cases differing philosophies and expectations may lead the mentor teacher or the teacher candidate into a different realm altogether, one that, as Graham (1993) points out, leads an individual "to question the certainty of [his or her] beliefs, to examine the assumptions underlying those beliefs and to arrive at judgments that result in new knowledge" (p. 214). One year I faced such a challenge.

COMPETING PHILOSOPHIES

I believe in a student-centered, teacher-as-facilitator, literature-as-discovery approach to teaching. I saw myself as modeling all these things for my teacher candidate and being willing to learn from him and "steal" many of his ideas that would fit snugly into my set perceptions of teaching as it should be. Instead, I was confronted with someone who believed primarily in the teacher-centered, lecture-oriented approach with which he was comfortable and from which he had learned and benefited as a student. I could remember those kinds of courses, literature seminars with 12 English majors completely engrossed in examining the foils in Shakespearean plays. It was fun. It was invigorating. I loved it! Would it translate to my classroom in a rural, primarily farming, town where much of the population fell in the lower ranges of the socioeconomic spectrum? No way, I was sure. Then I wondered. The more I listened to the teacher candidate, the more I remembered my own experience, the more I began to question the wisdom and relevance of my own approach. Maybe I was shortchanging my kids; maybe I was depriving them of that scholarly experience of delving into discussions of motifs, themes, and symbols in the lecture format.

The questions this teacher candidate raised were different from those with which I had become comfortable. He seriously and thoughtfully questioned the student-centered approach I was sure was the answer. Reluctantly, I agreed that there were very traditional, teacher-centered instructors in our building and, probably, in our mentor group that the teacher candidate could observe in addition to observing me. He did observe others teaching, and he came back with even more questions. Teacher-centered classrooms can be much quieter than my classroom usually is, and he wondered if it wasn't possible that students were less likely to be distracted in quieter environments. He observed that there might be more rigor and depth in lecture format classes than in a class where students were peer editing and responding and expressing their individual opinions. He taught lessons that were more student-centered, to please me I'm sure, and then he tried out the more comfortable, to him, lecture and teacher-led discussion format. As I watched him attempt to engage the students in the way I had been taught in English classes in college, I began to question intensely my own approach.

REVISING FAMILIAR TENSIONS

To be certain, I had grappled with these same worries before: once when I first started teaching and was afraid that what I had been taught in teacher education classrooms wouldn't translate into public high schools (because I had been told it wouldn't); and once when I left teaching for a 2-year term and then returned to the profession scared and uncertain that I still "had it." Here I was again, worried that what I had been doing for years was wrong. Will we ever get it right? I wondered.

I watched, I listened. I thought. I prayed. I went back to the basics. I reread Rosenblatt (1968); Tchudi and Tchudi (1991); and Kirby, Liner, and Vinz (1988). I took a harder, closer look at Foster (1994) and Atwell (1987). I thought. I even lectured for a few days. It didn't feel good. It felt forced. My students looked puzzled. I wrote about my thoughts in my journal:

> Who am I? I know I don't have all the answers, but I thought I had more than I think I have now. What is the right thing for these kids? What is the best approach for reaching these young people? What matters most to them? A teacher-certified "right answer" or a truth they've discovered for themselves?

I had long believed that we retain more of what we discover for ourselves. Ownership of our learning experience is more likely to take place when we experience new information in a way that makes it ours through discovery (Joyce & Weil, 1980). I knew that before I started my experience with the collaborative inquiry group of mentor teachers, but I knew it only academically. Through the long, dark period of self-doubt and the challenging period of self-examination, I "discovered" again for myself—in a way I could internalize and assume ownership of—that teaching is, for me, student-centered and teacher-facilitated.

It was a painful process. It was a struggle, but it was amazingly fun. Real growth took place in me this past year, and not just in the sense that I affirmed what I already believed to be true. I was forced to see myself as others saw me and question if what others were seeing was valid and reasonable. I had to become an objective evaluator of my own teaching in a way that I had not done for a long time. I reflect every day. I evaluate in my head on my drive home what went well and what didn't, but I had not seriously looked at myself through the lens of the camera in a long time. I have videotaped my teaching for staff development courses and been comfortable doing it. I had not, however, videotaped myself and watched to see if I believed in what was taking place. I had never watched to see if I sincerely believed that real learning was taking place, to see if the students were truly involved and engaged and, I now wondered, if my students were becoming learners through my approach.

Over the summer I had developed a year-long project for my seniors that involved the quest theme in literature. I looked, now, at the beginning of those projects. Initially, the students had read *Le Morte D'Arthur* together and then chosen whether to read *The Once and Future King* by T. H. White or *The Hollow Hills* by Mary Stewart. The students kept reading logs and process logs, interviewed community contact people of their choosing about five of ten different aspects of the personal quest (for fame, wealth, financial security, emotional stability, and so forth), and transcribed the interviews in their journals. The students also went to the computer lab and completed a Georgia Career Information Series (GCIS) inventory to match their own interests and abilities with possible careers. This was the first 6-week phase of the project. I picked up the students' journals and began flipping through them. I read such comments as, "This is the first time I've seen a valid connection between the literature we have to read in class and something that matters to me in the immediate present." Another student wrote:

> If Arthur was faced with this many challenges, no wonder I'm having a hard time making up my mind what to do with my life after I graduate. I guess it really is okay to be undecided right now. I'm glad I had to read these books and think about them in connection with myself. I'd never done that before.

In my journal I wrote:

> The students seem to be benefiting from the approach I believe in. I loved what S. said about thinking about the books in connection with her own life. That's what I want to see happen. But what if I'm wrong? What if I should be having them write more traditional literary analysis instead of analyzing those works through their responses?

Even though I had seen students quote more examples from the literary texts and comment more specifically on them through this project than I had ever seen before in a five-paragraph composition format, I was still uncertain because of the presence of this other, questioning person in my room.

Not only did he ask the simple things such as, "How did you come up with this idea," but he also wondered if the students were truly making meaning of the text or if they were merely thinking about their own immediate lives in a more complex format. Did they, he wondered, understand the complex dynamics of a quest motif, had they understood the machinations of Arthur's kingdom? Were they coming to literature in such a way that would allow them to engage in "close readings" of future texts? Were they learning?

ADDRESSING UNCERTAINTIES THROUGH TEACHER RESEARCH

As the year progressed, the relationship between my teacher candidate and me grew very tense. The more he questioned and seemed to reject a pedagogy I believed was right for students, the more I felt personally threatened. Of course, there were other factors that entered into the dynamics, such as school politics and career questions for both of us, but our relationship was strained. After he had been teaching for some time and had taught lessons in all four of the preparations he had assumed, we split the classes. He kept two and I took two back. At this point, I decided to engage in a little teacher research. Admittedly, I was biased toward teaching as facilitating and student discovery. That bias may have affected what followed in my teacher research. On the other hand, at this point in time, I was thoroughly confused and extremely unsettled. At one time in my career, I had been a comfortable transmitter of knowledge—perhaps that would be okay again. At any rate, certainly biased and certainly anxious, I proceeded with some action research.

At the time, I was a strong believer in Models of Teaching (Joyce & Weil, 1980). I had taken staff development courses in this approach to teaching and also had taken the training to be a Models instructor. One of the underlying principles of the Models of Teaching approach is that students need to learn strategies that help them become independent learners. Many times when students encounter new material, they are forced to weed out extraneous material and information to determine the characteristics of a concept in order to truly master it. One of the models, Concept Attainment, is an approach to learning that strategy. My teacher research into my own practice and my students' learning was organized around doing two different lessons on the concept of slanted writing. I planned to do one lesson using the Models of Teaching Concept Attainment approach and one using a standard lecture format.

I had two sections of a senior class whose curriculum called for mastery of the concept of slanted writing. (The lesson that follows is one I adapted from one developed by the Augusta teaching cadre in Augusta, Georgia, and presented in their Models of Teaching training seminar.) In the Concept Attainment class, I began with a data set of sentences selected from newspapers. The sentences were examples of slanted writing, straight news leads, and sports leads. The data set included sentences such as: "1. Braves Slam Dodgers" and "2. Bulldogs Win Season Opener." In the lesson, following the procedure established in the Models of Teaching procedure for a Concept Attainment lesson, I call each of the sentences a positive or negative exemplar of the concept we are investigating. Sentences that illustrate the concept to be attained are called "positive exemplars," and sentences that are not examples of that concept are "negative exemplars." The goal is to have students begin to think about what characterizes a positive exemplar. A full data set should appear to have many possible solutions when the activity begins. In order to encourage multiple levels of thinking, the lesson aims to have students consider a wide range of possibilities and to think deeply about what they see as common characteristics. Gradually, the facilitator indicates more and more negative exemplars, weeding out more of the possibilities, which necessitates the students' reconceptualizing their thinking and reformulating possibilities. Ultimately, as students begin to determine what they believe the characteristics of the positive exemplars are, the facilitator asks students to suggest some of the positive and negative exemplars.

I asked the students to read over the list of sentences, or exemplars, and start thinking about common denominators. I provided a data set to include possible categories for early contemplation of type styles, different fonts, good news, sports story headlines, and, of course, slanted writing. Initially, I knew, they would focus on the fonts of the sentences, as I had typed all of the sentences in various styles of type, not to confuse them but to encourage critical thinking by having them consider a wide range of possibilities for common characteristics. Following the procedure for Concept Attainment lessons, I asked students to focus on sentences in the data set that I, as facilitator, said were positive exemplars. Students must forget about the negative exemplars once sentences are so identified in order to focus on the common characteristics of the remaining sentences and not be confused by trying to see if the negatives have something in common as well. The facilitator calls out numbers of sentences, identifying each of the sentences in the data set as either negative or positive. For instance, in the examples I provided above, the facilitator would identify sentence one, "Braves Slam Dodgers" as positive. If students are beginning to list characteristics that indicate the concept is sports story headlines, the facilitator guides them to reconfigure their list by identifying sentence two, "Bulldogs Win Season Opener," as a negative exemplar. Concentrating only on the attributes of the positive examples, the students finally see that all of the positives are examples of writing that is biased, or slanted.

Throughout the lesson, students work with a partner. The teacher provides ample time for discussion and reflection as the lesson progresses. As we progressed through the data set, students were asked to work with their partners and consider what common attributes they could find within the positive exemplars only, formulate a hypothesis, and test that hypothesis with an attempt to select for themselves a positive exemplar. We worked through the remainder of the data set, with students wildly waving their hands to suggest a positive exemplar. Finally, when all of the positives had been identified, I asked the students, again working with a partner, to jot down all of the attributes that they had discovered were common for the positives. Students wrote down such characteristics as "strong verbs," "forceful language," "writer's viewpoint is obvious," and so forth. As I made my way around the room, I could determine that every set of partners had listed the majority of the attributes of slanted writing. I had the partners call out the attributes, and we recorded them on the board. Then I asked them what they understood to be true from the attributes they had listed. What followed was a description of slanted writing better than one I had ever read in a textbook! I told them the concept was called "slanted writing," and they immediately began talking about the uses of such writing, the manipulation behind such writing, and the responsibilities of the reader when he or she encounters such writing. On their own, they offered examples of having been fooled by such writing when they had accepted it as fact because of the medium in which they encountered it. They talked about the number of sports leads that contained slanted writing and justified it in that context with explanations of hometown newspapers using slanted writing to encourage a healthy bias in support of hometown teams. They continued with a loud discussion of how that same approach was wrong when discussing a presidential press conference.

Later, when the students were asked to write about slanted writing in an assessment situation, this class was able to fluently and intelligently discuss and evaluate different types of slanted writing. Moreover, students frequently returned to a discussion of this lesson as they read different things throughout the year. Often, they would bring in newspapers or news magazines and point out the slanted writing. They would insert loaded, or slanted, language in persuasive essays and, in conferences with me later, point out their use of the loaded words. None of this happened in the class that I lectured to about slanted writing.

In the lecture class, I deliberately structured a transmission lesson in order to contrast for myself my own strengths and weaknesses as well as to observe student behaviors in a transmission setting. I consciously chose not to employ strategies such as brainstorming, small group discussion, or any other student-centered activity. The reason behind that obviously crucial choice was that I was trying to replicate for myself the kind of teaching I believed my teacher candidate found so compelling. Our earlier discussions about his perceptions of effective teaching led me to believe that he valued a quiet classroom, with the teacher providing the essential information and students contributing to the classroom by answering teacher-generated "closed" questions (Beach & Marshall, 1991).

Essentially, I gave the students the same information that their peers had discovered for themselves. I made overhead transparencies of the sentences that had been my positive exemplars for the other class. I put each sentence on a separate transparency and put the transparencies on the overhead one at a time. I called on student volunteers to read the sentences and asked students to explain what the sentences were saying. Pointedly, I cautioned them to ignore the font and typeface and concentrate on the content of the sentence. I asked students to explain what "Braves Slam Dodgers" meant. Naturally, the students answered that the Braves won the ball game. I asked them what the sentence would mean if it had said, "Braves Win Season Opener Against Los Angeles." Again, the students replied that it would still mean that the Braves had won the ball game.

After we went through each of the examples I had generated, "discussing" the meanings of the sentences, I specifically told them that we were looking at examples of slanted writing. I gave them a definition and asked them to record that definition and at least two examples from our discussion in their notebooks. I warned a test was in the offing and gave specific examples of slanted writing, how it is used, how it is misused, when it is acceptable, and when it is reprehensible. I even offered the examples of acceptable slanted writing (hometown sports stories) generated by the other class. Basically, the two classes had the same exact information. In one class, students had discovered the information for themselves and thus had ownership of the concept. In the other class, I had given the information to the students, and they had studied it for a test; however, unlike their peers in the other class, they never returned to slanted writing in either their discussions of writing or in their own writing. I believed they had no real-long term comprehension of how the concept worked.

CONSIDERING THE IMPLICATIONS

At this point, it is probably important to note that another teacher utilizing the same procedure may have encountered completely different results. It is also possible that the differences in the two classes themselves account for the differences in the long-term results of carryover into future discussions and writings. It is conceivable that I found what I wanted to find. I am not arguing that I was a researcher completely free of bias or vested interests. However, I must say again that I was anxious and less certain of myself and my practice than I had been a year earlier. The honest questions that my teacher candidate was raising, his personal stories of having been turned on to learning through rigorous lecture and guided questioning formats in his own educational experience, and his thoughtful observations of the difference in noise levels (and possible increases of potential for concentration) between teacher- and student-centered classrooms had genuinely made me wonder, question, examine, and test my own assumptions. Even though my teacher research into my students and their slanted writing study led me to believe that I was doing the right thing for them at this particular point in time, I was very aware that a different unit of study, a different set of students, or even a different time in the academic year could alter those results.

Through the challenge offered by my teacher candidate, I was forced to carefully examine my own practice and the huge set of assumptions undergirding that practice. Never again will I take for granted that what I think I know about my students and my practice is always best. There might be a student in my classroom who would thrive as much under a lecture format as my teacher candidate had in his academic career. His questioning and his explanation of his experiences forced me into an awareness that will keep those possibilities in the forefront of my thinking about my classroom.

I found for myself what I hope to provide for my students: that real learning takes place when you discover for yourself, through close examination and real interaction, some essential truth that you can possess and take home with you. Yes, students do retain more when they discover new material for themselves. Yes, real learning takes place. Yes, they become engaged and learn and value (sometimes) the experience.

I can attest to real teaching and real learning taking place in a setting where the activities are natural evolutions of the objectives and not activities for the sake of having an activity. I came to passionately assert that there is a difference between providing a meaningful learning experience and "extending a lesson because we feel somewhat that we're supposed to" (Altwerger, 1991, p. 20).

I became a student again. I became a researcher. I became a student of my own practices, a student of students and a researcher of belief versus practice. Because of the challenges of working closely for an entire school year with a teacher candidate with different beliefs from my own, I moved from being a teacher to becoming a student again. I probably would not have made such a move at this point in time if it had not been for the drastic difference in philosophy I faced. It is a move I hope will be ongoing as I continue to work with the collaborative community we've built. I know there are others who struggle with the same issues, others who are determined to improve their own practice and who are willing to be brutally honest about the shortcomings and difficulties they face as they improve their teaching. It is a refreshing change of pace to know that there is an honest desire to improve and better one's teaching without risk of being judged and found incompetent by the person next door. Being a part of a supportive collaborative community led me to take a fresh look at myself, my practice, my philosophy, and my background. The initial tensions between my teacher candidate and me led to productive growth for me as an educator.

REFERENCES

Altwerger, B. (1991). Whole language teachers: Empowered professionals. In J. Hydrick (Ed.), *Whole language: Empowerment at the chalk face* (pp. 15–29). New York: Scholastic.

Atwell, N. (1987). *In the middle: Writing, reading, and learning with adolescents.* Portsmouth, NH: Boynton/Cook.

Beach, R., & Marshall, J. (1991). *Teaching literature in the secondary school.* San Diego: Harcourt Brace Jovanovich.

Foster, H. M. (1994). *Crossing over: Whole language for secondary English teachers.* Fort Worth, TX: Harcourt Brace College Publishers.

Graham, P. (1993). Curious positions: Reciprocity and tensions in the student teacher/cooperating teacher relationship. *English Education, 25*(4), 213–230.

Joyce, B., & Weil, M. (1980). *Models of teaching* (3rd ed.). Englewood Cliffs, NJ: Prentice-Hall.

Kirby, D., Liner, T., & Vinz, R. (1988). *Inside out: Developmental strategies for teaching writing* (2nd ed.). Portsmouth, NH: Boynton/Cook.

Rosenblatt, L. (1968). *Literature as exploration* (3rd ed.). New York: Noble & Noble.

Tchudi, S. N., & Tchudi, S. J. (1991). *The English/language arts handbook: Classroom strategies for teachers.* Portsmouth, NH: Boynton/Cook.

PART II

Teacher Research in a Collaborative Inquiry Community

We would be less than honest if we did not admit that the thought of doing classroom research was initially a frightening possibility to most of the mentor teachers in our group. We openly (and secretly) feared statistical data, incalculable formulas, and incomprehensible results. What we came to realize in the early years of our work together, however, was that our fears were unfounded. We learned to trust the ethnography of our own classrooms, students, and experiences.

Nothing more clearly reveals that trust than the multiple perspectives represented in these chapters. Chapter 6 discusses specifically how teacher candidates, through a variety of projects instigated through their university courses (with key input from mentor teachers), research and discover crucial information about themselves and their students as readers, writers, and learners. In the process, they naturally assume the persona and the confidence of real researchers, who honestly seek answers to real questions about students and their learning.

The remaining chapters in this part of the book include very specific research questions grounded in the classroom experiences and dilemmas of the teacher candidates, their mentor teachers, and a wide range of students. Chapter 7 contrasts avid and reluctant writers, whose experiences are revealed in personal interviews conducted and analyzed by the teacher candidates. Chapter 8 focuses on the reading preferences and habits of high school students and how one teacher candidate used small group book shares to challenge and encourage students to read independently and for pleasure. Chapter 9 details how a behavior journal helped a teacher candidate gain new understanding of the connections between student behavior, teacher behavior, and the often uncontrollable factors in a classroom setting. Finally, Chapter 10 represents a model research collaboration between a teacher candidate, her mentor teacher, and their students.

In all of this research there is evidence of the collaborative nature of our community and the value we place on teacher research. The research questions often are negotiated by teacher candidates, mentor teachers, and university faculty. We share results and insight; we reconceptualize our roles as educators; we act on our findings. Above all, we choose to continue the research each year as our group expands to admit new faces and new questions.

CHAPTER 6

Teacher Candidate Research on Literacy in High School Classrooms

Peg Graham & Sally Hudson-Ross

With mentor teachers and the class of 1994–95, Peg and Sally devised teacher research projects to help teacher candidates explore their students' insights into literacy learning. Four projects and how they were developed are described here. As teacher candidates read textbooks on campus, they also collected data on the same topic at school. Graduates consistently report that the projects help them hear student voices and know their students as individuals. Although the projects change across the years as we learn more and raise new questions, the concept of learning to teach from our students remains a centerpiece of our classrooms, both on campus and in schools.

In "The Devil and Research," Richard Lloyd-Jones (1986) defines a researcher as "merely a person who looks very carefully and then reports very carefully what has been seen so that others will believe it is a useful way of looking" (p. 5). As teacher educators who are interested in the concept of "learning to teach," we want to promote these ways of looking and reporting among our teacher candidates, the mentor teachers who work with them, and ourselves. Teacher research experiences enable us to make sense of the events in our classrooms, offering us opportunities to confront our preconceptions about how to organize learning for students and question how we have constructed our theories.

Lortie (1975) and others write about the "apprenticeship of observation"—the fact that we all learn to teach by having been students ourselves—which influences the images, beliefs, and theories of teaching brought to teacher education programs by preservice teachers. In many cases, these theories are based on a narrow band of experiences and stories, particularly if the teacher candidates' school experiences were limited to the honors track, for example. In our experience, these theories are sometimes so strong that teacher candidates (and experienced teachers too) choose their facts to fit their theories, washing out the influence of professional literature and research. Also, these theories often are based on personal histories and biographical data or institutional constraints, which means they may not add up to a coherent theory of learning but instead become a set of competing or eclectic theories. As a result, we believe it is important to invite teacher candidates to look carefully at learners and classrooms, to report thoughtfully what they have seen, and to determine how those practical experiences modify the theories they bring with them as they undertake the complex process of learning to become teachers.

We begin our fall classes with four classroom-based projects that teacher candidates carry out in their schools. Each project is designed to build teacher candidate research skills. Our major goal is to connect what they are reading at the university with what they are experiencing in the public school classroom in order to create a link between theory and practice and to emphasize how practice modifies theory. A year-long placement gives teacher candidates ample time to conduct their research, become familiar with their students, acquaint themselves with the class curriculum, and establish a professional working relationship with their mentor teachers. We hope that by conducting research focused on the students in their classrooms, teacher candidates will learn how to observe children and make important curricular and instructional decisions throughout their careers.

To make sure that we did not simply impose an agenda on the teacher candidates that would disrupt mentor teachers' classrooms, we negotiated with the mentor teachers the kinds of research experiences most important for teacher candidates to have.

BECOMING TEACHER RESEARCHERS: PROCESS AND PRODUCT

In each of four research projects, teacher candidates used a different type of classroom-research methodology to acquire information from students. We suggested methods that would render useful data for each of the four projects, but teacher candidates could expand their data sources if they wished. After collecting data for a particular project, teacher candidates returned to the university setting to share and analyze their information. Part of that information was taken from autobiographical profiles in which the teacher candidates focused on their own experiences as learners within adolescent culture, as readers, and as writers in secondary schools. By incorporating these personal inquiries into the classroom research, teacher candidates were able to compare and contrast their personal histories with their students'

Left to right, Angela Hodges, Peg Graham, and Bill Gabelhausen discuss data collection methods.

experience while also investigating the sources of the theories influencing their images of teacher.

Our intention was to structure the assignments enough that teacher candidates would have similar types of information to categorize, compare, and contrast in their analyses. As teacher candidates gained more experience and confidence with the role of researcher, we relinquished more and more of the process to them. The final project on reading culminated in teacher candidates devising a method of data analysis they thought would be more efficient and effective, based on their experiences with the three preceding research projects.

Project 1: Adolescent Culture/Students and Self

The first project had two parts. In phase one, we asked teacher candidates to write a profile of themselves as learners, pushing them to reflect on how they perceived themselves as learners within the cultures of adolescence and high school.

The second phase of the project directed teacher candidates to interview students about their lives within the culture of school and adolescence. The assignment we gave them offered ideas for the kinds of information teacher candidates might try to elicit from students:

> Interview student(s) about their lives within the culture of school and adolescence. Write a student profile or a set of student profiles. You might consider the following questions:
> - What influences those students?
> - With which groups or cliques do they identify?
> - What blocks or facilitates their learning and sense of well-being?
> - What patterns emerge across the adolescent profiles we compile?
> - How are those patterns different from or similar to the patterns you have identified as influential on your own adolescence and high school experience?
> - Of what importance are these insights to teaching and learning in specific schools/classrooms?

Although we indicated the kind of information they should try to glean, teacher candidates created interview questions on their own, experimenting with questions that prompted elaboration from interviewees and structured versus semistructured formats. From those interviews, teacher candidates wrote one or more student profiles, which they shared with other teacher candidates.

The discussion and analysis of the data were not formally structured at this point, but teacher candidates were asked to identify recurrent themes and patterns of response, which they reflected on in their dialogue journals. Some teacher candidates, such as Jennifer McDuffie Stewart, were convinced that interviewing students offered teachers an array of benefits. Jennifer wrote:

> Talking to young people one-on-one like this really helped me get a feel for the variety of teenager problems, preferences, and perceptions I'd be facing. Of course, this was a tremendous help when I began planning my lessons for the class. I knew the *individual students* who would be participants in those lessons; I wasn't just planning for a random group of tenth graders.
>
> As an interviewer, I gave interviewees my undivided attention for a mere 10 minutes—and yet it altered the way they viewed me as a person. My students were flattered by the attention: after all, it's not often they get so much time from a teacher (unless they've done something "bad"). This was positive attention focused completely on the individual's feelings and interests. As a result, I had a few allies in the class before I even began teaching, a situation that definitely made me feel more at ease. . . . [For example], although Jake initially responded to

my interview questions as a sort of joke, after a few questions asking for his opinion, he abandoned the wisecracks, [and] assumed a more polite demeanor. . . . Serious conversation with a caring adult embarrassed him somewhat. However, it also became clear to me that Jake enjoyed being able to talk about himself to someone who really listened.

Project 2: Student Discourse/Language

The courses we team teach include a class in language issues for teachers. To raise topics such as teaching Standard English and fostering respect for the language variations of students, we asked teacher candidates to audiotape student conversations in the cafeteria, the classroom, or the hallways so that they could study students' language in different situations. Teacher candidates audiotaped or videotaped talk among one or more groups of students in situations that ranged from very formal to relatively informal exchanges. With the assistance of the students who participated in the exchanges, teacher candidates transcribed 5–10-minute excerpts from the talk. In an extended journal entry, teacher candidates analyzed the transcription data, using the following questions, which we had devised to prompt their reflections on the data:

- What are the characteristics of the participants in the conversation you taped? [location; age, education, sex, social position; racial/ethnic identity; other characteristics]
- What was the occasion for the conversation? Upon what topics did the participants focus?
- Do they use identifiable genres? [stories, jokes, prayers, admonitions, insults]
- What distinguishes the students' language and dialect from that of the mainstream culture? Be specific. Note diction, syntax, sentence structure, etc. Of what importance is that dialect to the students? Why?
- What can the students say about the etymology of particular terms? What terms were unfamiliar to you?
- What community values or aspects of community culture seem to be represented in this conversation? In what ways is the language they are using inclusive or exclusive?
- What do you notice about patterns of language use across individuals participating in the conversation? What variations? Commonalities?
- Of what importance is all of this information to understanding your students, their language facility, and their language needs?
- How can you use those insights to serve you in the classroom? What implications does it have for what you teach and how you teach it?

- Of what value would it have been to have students assist in the transcription process? or Why was it helpful to have students assist in the transcription process?

With partners, teacher candidates noted language patterns across their own and peers' samples, striving to make connections and appreciate the usefulness of sharing findings with fellow researchers. After collecting transcript data and journal entries about language patterns from all of the teacher researchers, Sally and Peg selected and printed up excerpts from all of the samples, clustering them under category headings as a model for how teacher candidates might organize data. For example, the following is a sample of the data compiled about *informal talk:*

> In informal talk, students take on and fulfill different speaker roles (i.e., instigator, orchestrator, comic, reinforcer, storyteller, interpreter), which relate to both their personalities and the group's dynamic.

> In one conversation, the males tended to ask questions and leave the floor open for jokes, effectively directing the conversation in spite of one female participant's efforts to bring in her viewpoints.

> "You know," "I mean," and "like" overpopulate students' informal conversations.

> Informal dialogue sometimes reflects a hierarchy among the participants, with power being placed in the hands of those who set the standards for turn-taking and on-task behaviors.

> During informal conversation, speakers understand ambiguous statements due to the context for their talk.

> In informal talk, speakers sharing a common context and experience don't explain all of their references.

In later years, as we continued to refine assignments, we combined this language-focused project with opportunities to shadow students through their school days.

Project 3: Student Writers/Self as Writer

As teacher candidates gained experience with conducting research, we expanded their options for methods and sources of data and imposed more structure on analyzing the data they brought back to the university. As always, we asked teacher candidates to think about their own experiences as

Figure 6.1. Sample writing data analysis.

Look at and talk through all of your interviews and student papers. As you do, keep a jot list of things that strike you or that you notice. When you are finished, list here the main points that strike you. Be VERY specific; if possible, quote your data exactly as we did in Language Project Excerpts. Write clearly enough for a typist to copy your words.

What strikes you? What do you notice?	**As a result of what you noticed, what advice would you give teachers of writing?**
Students usually revised their writing after its completion (if student corrects as he/she writes, he/she has very little problem with control and fluency).	Teachers must realize that it's easier for students who correct as they write and revise afterwards than vice versa. For students who revise afterwards, the fluency may be stunted if they are forced to revise during the project.
Students enjoy having their work displayed (and excerpts read) for/to others.	Teachers should try to find good points in students' writing to share with class, thus allowing feedback.
Trying to write in one sitting can cause frustration and stop fluency.	Writing should be a long-term assignment; it should be a process that students can build on.

writers before asking them to investigate their students as writers. Working from different data sources—writing samples and interviews of more proficient and less proficient student writers, and their own writers' autobiographies—individual teacher candidates worked with partners to analyze the data.

We provided a chart with two columns that structured how teacher candidates would select and record important data (see Figure 6.1). We emphasized that they should quote directly from the data as we had modeled for them with the Language Research Project. They selected excerpts from their data that they deemed important and wrote them down on blocks in column 1 on the blank chart. Then coupled with a partner, they combined their data and devised advice for writing teachers implied by their findings. The advice was recorded in column 2. In addition to discovering overlaps in what their data revealed about more and less proficient student writers, the teacher researchers collaborated on making the teacherly turn toward implications for practice, a turn that facilitated their shift from student to teacher.

When they had completed their charts, teacher candidates turned in their findings and their advice to us. We compiled all of the excerpts and advice in a chart we typed up and then returned to the teacher candidates, asking them to read all of the data and implications from all of their classmates before writing marginalia (notes in the margins of the charts as they connected points), a means of discovering main points and trends across all of the samples. Immersing themselves in the data this way provided them with perspectives from every teacher researcher in the class. As a culminating activity, we asked teacher candidates to write an extended journal entry rather than some sort of formal report. We hoped they would be able to express their insights in ways that would help them to apply the findings to their own students and classrooms.

Teacher candidates organized their reflections in many different ways in the extended journal, but Bill Gabelhausen's list of "Common Threads" at the end of his entry offers a sample of the kinds of insights they derived from the research:

Common Threads

The following are common threads or thoughts that surfaced throughout the data. Some of these threads did not surprise me, while others caught me off guard.

1. *Free choice*—I've talked about the issue before, so I won't elaborate. I thought this idea might surface in the data. Students want some significant *amount of control.* I think this is a wonderful thing because it may heighten interest, develop a voice, and create works that the student is willing to spend a significant amount of time with. We can use this tool, but we have to be careful not to abuse it or become a victim of its power.

2. *Computers*—There is not a whole lot to be said about this one. Computers are becoming the pen and paper of this generation. I am not 100% computer competent so that's a drawback. But I am learning. The students at CSHS help me with the computer in Beth's room. They get a real kick out of helping a future teacher.

3. *Exhibiting works*—All students, regardless of ability, like to see their work on exhibition. This leads directly to my last two points: insecurity/pride.

4. *Insecurity and lack of pride*—This is the one that surprised me. (These are not meant to be statements. Not all of the students exhibit these qualities.) Even the most advanced writer, along with the least proficient, shows a substantial amount of insecurity and lack of pride in their writing. I think this is due to the following factors:

    a. Writing is *personal.* It is concrete evidence of one's thoughts. Writers fear judgments of right or wrong, and good or bad. At the high school age, students are discovering a lot about themselves and to translate those discoveries to paper would be wonderful, but extremely risky for that age.

    b. We, as students, have not been guided/pushed/shoved down avenues involving creativity or imagination. We *have been taught to use formulas* in writing, formulas that dictate right or wrong. Instead of standing back, reading a piece of your writing, and saying, "Yes! That's great! That is exactly how I feel at this moment in time," we usually reread our piece, checking our adherence to format, structure, and saying, "What will the teacher think when she reads this?"

    c. I think I discovered something very interesting in our data collection sheets. Our word choice subtly differs in the "advice to teachers" section in regards to less proficient and more proficient writers.

5. *The language we use. Less Proficient Writers*—I see the word *encourage* over and over again. This supports the role of the teacher. We must let these less avid writers know that we are on their side. We want them to do their best, we will support them along the process, we will guide them out of dead-end streets or trouble areas; we will let them know that it is okay to get "stuck" or "lost." We are part of the support team. *More Proficient Writers*—With this group of writers we use words like *engage, stress,* and *clarify.* We, as teachers, take on a more active role. We challenge the students to challenge themselves. We allow them to explore the nooks and crannies of the process. We push them toward a clear voice and/or style.

I learned a lot via [these] data. However, it will be nice to set it aside for a little while. I feel overloaded in the brain department. I'm not sure if I can write about writing for a couple days. Hopefully, writing about reading will be a different story.

In Chapter 7, other teacher candidates explain their experiences writing profiles of student writers, an angle we explored more thoroughly in our second year of the experimental program.

Project 4: Student Readers/Self as Reader

Teacher candidates anticipated their Reading Research Project with an air of confidence they had not had at the beginning of the quarter. As had become our habit, we assigned an autobiographical profile of the teacher candidate as a reader before launching into research on student readers. Embedded within the directions for the reading autobiography were explicit statements about how the profile would contribute to the database we would create for the whole class of teacher candidate researchers. Again, we wanted to offer teacher candidates more control over how they designed their studies. As a group we discussed what kind of questions we had about student readers and their reading habits, the kinds of data that would inform our research questions, and the methods of data collection that would render the information we sought. Teacher candidates decided that reading surveys and interviews with students about reading would be most fruitful. Most of the teacher candidates had become convinced of the power of asking directly for student input and had good examples of surveys their teachers had administered about reading interests at the beginning of the school year. Some opted to use those existing data. Others opted to design another reading survey to get more specific or different kinds of data. This time we needed no assignment sheet dictating what to do: Teacher candidates had begun to take ownership of the research they conducted.

Based on their prior experience with research, teacher candidates were asked to brainstorm a list of ideas about how to approach the reading research project most productively. Throughout that discussion, they focused most pointedly on the analysis stage, seeking to streamline their approach to making sense of the data they compiled. They came up with the following list of ideas for that phase of their research:

- Use "chart blocks" again (to control for overwriting), but add a heading or label to each to facilitate organizing the data and discovering patterns.
- Put the name of each researcher on the excerpts to facilitate referral to specific data and to identify the original researcher for verification or elaboration of data.
- Meet with a second pair of researchers and label data excerpts together.
- Use separate strips of paper for the chart blocks so similar headings can be grouped together more easily.
- Cluster related excerpts/chart blocks from each researcher group by patterns and type.
- Continue to use marginalia as a means to identify trends across data samples.

Teacher candidates went to their school classrooms to administer the surveys they devised and to conduct individual and small group interviews. Then teacher candidates returned to the university to analyze the data they had collected: autobiographies, surveys, transcripts of interviews, even a videotape of one small group. In pairs, teacher candidates compared their findings. As they talked, they wrote down on slips of paper the important excerpts that emerged from the data. Gradually, they exhausted all of the data and reached all insights they could. Then each pair joined another pair of teacher candidates and shared their findings. When both groups detected a similar pattern, they grouped those data together under a single heading such as "School Reading Assignments vs. Pleasure Reading" or "Gender Preferences" or "Text Selection."

Gradually, over 3 hours, teacher candidates made sense of their data and added to each pattern an implication for teachers. We collected their work and typed it up in a chart, which we again distributed to all of the teacher candidates. Because these teacher researchers had learned to organize their data more efficiently, the process of reflecting on those findings was also easier. Again they wrote marginal comments on the chart and wrote about their discoveries in their dialogue journals, directing their attention to what these findings implied for their classroom practice. A sampling of those journal entries indicates what they theorized about readers and students' experiences with literature in school:

> There are trends which succeeding generations of students follow . . . it was not just Nick and my own reader biographies which were similar to the students at our respective high schools, it was everyone's. Regardless of school, level, or any other factor, the observations . . . demonstrate at least two ideas: students read what they find interesting, and students seem to develop in stages or phases. (Mace Gunter)

> My one belief left standing firm after reading the "Insights" about readers is that *anybody,* no matter what kind of background they have or academic skill level they're at, can be a lover of reading if they meet with the right book at the right time. . . . The other major issue which concerns me is helping students choose literature that's appropriate and appealing to them. I'm afraid my knowledge is very limited, and it's difficult to know what might just fit. (Clare Marks [pseudonym])

> I realized something that at least partially explained the distaste for reading that I had encountered in so many students. Many of the students said they don't like to read, and would then say something about

how they liked to read Stephen King books or books about art, etc. It's almost like they think if they don't like to read "classics," they don't like to read at all.

This really opened my eyes to what was going on in the classroom. Students who were reading magazines, newspapers, 500-page John Grisham books, etc., were claiming to be nonreaders, because what they read was entertaining and not "worthy" of being taught in school. *I am still not sure what exactly can be done to change this attitude, but I feel strongly that letting students choose their own books to read in and for school is a step in the right direction.* While this is not an ultimate solution, it is a way to send students the message that all books are important, not just those written by authors such as Shakespeare and Melville. I know that there is a time and place for these classics, but at the same time, I strongly believe that it will take much more than those to turn a nonreader on to reading. (Jennifer McDuffie Stewart)

Jennifer took off on her commitment to independent reading in her own research project, which she reports here in Chapter 9.

In more recent years, with less secretarial and copying support, students have worked quite efficiently from handwritten charts of findings passed among groups. We also have come to realize that individual stories are uniquely important findings, more important to teachers than the patterns we sought in our earlier work.

In addition, both teacher candidates and their mentor partners, such as Amy Wilbourne and Christina Healan (see Chapter 10), emerged with a well-developed teacher research mind-set that shaped their thinking about what constitutes good classroom research. Amy and Christina even wrote up their own set of recommendations for good research based on their experiences with these projects (see Figure 6.2).

CONCLUSION

Although our teacher candidates were placed in six different schools in five different school districts that served extremely different communities, their research with students supported what we had been reading in the professional literature. For example, the Reading Research Projects strongly supported teaching reading and literature that is attuned to student needs and interests, offers students choices, and is purposeful. The student readers emphasized how important parents and friends are as influences on their reading, and students offered insights into how to teach in supportive and chal-

Figure 6.2. Recommendations for good research, by Christina Healan (mentor partner) and Amy Wilbourne (teacher candidate).

___

Questions

Open-ended (versus yes/no) questions yield more interesting interview data.

Structuring questions for an interview is good; however, be open to following a student's lead into related areas.

Avoid leading questions—"I liked clubs. Do you?"

Data collection/methods (credibility, reliability, validity)

The more sources of data, generally, the more believable will be the report.

The wider the range of students, generally, the more believable the report (unless uniqueness of a particular type is part of the questions, e.g., For what reasons do kids placed in gifted classes read popular literature?)

Analysis

In our class, strive for application: Given this finding or pattern, what will you do in a classroom as a result? (Be as specific as possible.)

Strive for depth of analysis. Go beyond a summary to thinking through alternative and possible interpretations. At the same time, don't overgeneralize beyond these data. If you interviewed six students, you can speak literally only about them, not all adolescents at a school.

Presentation

Include questions or other data collection information in a methods section or appendix so that the reader can assess what you did for him/herself.

Use pseudonyms for students (generally) to protect them from outside readers who may know their families, etc. (unless students specifically say in writing to use their names).

Number the pages of your report. (Makes feedback and discussion of your work easier.)

___

lenging ways. Given the preponderance of data they had collected as primary investigators in their own classrooms, teacher candidates expanded their experiences with learners different from themselves and in the process modified the theories that informed their images of what effective teachers do and how students learn.

The power of teacher research for teacher candidates is located in the voices of their students. Through formal and informal research methods that allowed them to see and hear their students more clearly, teacher candidates were able to revise assumptions and expectations they had brought to their teacher education program. As a result, these future teachers were able to connect the theoretical and the practical, exploring how one informs the other as they began to plan lessons for their first teaching experiences. Throughout the rest of the program, teacher candidates automatically returned to the research methods and mind-set they had been exposed to, as they assumed more and more responsibility for teaching, uncovering questions and dilemmas they could answer only by observing and listening to their students. They convinced themselves that teacher research was a "useful way of looking" and learning.

REFERENCES

Lloyd-Jones R. (1986). The devil and research. *Kansas English, 72*(1), 4–10.
Lortie, D. (1975). *Schoolteacher: A sociological study.* Chicago: University of Chicago Press.

FURTHER READING

Atwell, N. (1987). *In the middle: Writing, reading, and learning with adolescents.* Portsmouth, NH: Boynton/Cook.
Brown, D., & Rose, T. (1995). Self-reported classroom impact of teachers' theories about learning and obstacles to implementation. *Action in Teacher Education, 17*(1), 20–29.
Flanders, N., Bowyer, J., Ponzio, R., Ingvarson, L., Tisher, R., Lowery, L., & Reynolds, K. (1987). Support systems for teachers who form partnerships to help each other improve teaching. *Teacher Education Quarterly, 14*(3), 5–24.
Foster, H. M. (1994). *Crossing over: Whole language for secondary English teachers.* New York: Harcourt Brace.
Goodman, J. (1988a). Constructing a practical philosophy of teaching: A study of preservice teachers' professional perspectives. *Teaching and Teacher Education, 4*(2), 121–137.
Goodman, J. (1988b). University culture and the problem of reforming field experiences in teacher education. *Journal of Teacher Education, 29*(1), 45–53.

Grossman, P. (1990). *The making of a teacher: Teacher knowledge and teacher education.* New York: Teachers College Press.

Hubbard, R. S., & Power, B. M. (1993). *The art of classroom inquiry: A handbook for teacher-researchers.* Portsmouth, NH: Heinemann.

Kirby, D., & Liner, T., & Vinz, R. (1988). *Inside out: Developmental strategies for teaching writing* (2nd ed.). Portsmouth, NH: Boynton/Cook.

Mayher, J. (1990). *Uncommon sense: Theoretical practice in language education.* Portsmouth, NH: Heinemann.

Rodriguez, A. (1993). A dose of reality: Understanding the origin of the theory/practice dichotomy in teacher education from the students' point of view. *Journal of Teacher Education, 44*(3), 213–222.

Tobin, K. (1990). Changing metaphors and beliefs: A master switch for teaching? *Theory into Practice, 28,* 122–127.

Wiggins, R., & Clift, R. (1995). Oppositional pairs: Unresolved conflicts in student teaching. *Action in Teacher Education, 17*(1), 9–19.

CHAPTER 7

Case Studies of Ourselves and Student Writers

Heather Ivester, Jennifer Dail, Jenny Hart White, Katherine Hatcher, & Cheryl Protin Hancock

Jennifer Dail, Jenny Hart White, Katherine Hatcher, Heather Ivester, and Cheryl Protin Hancock share their research findings from case studies conducted with student writers. Their experiences gave all participants, both researchers and students, an opportunity to pause and reflect on the practices that encourage and discourage young writers. The advice they provide is informative for beginning and experienced teachers.

Wouldn't it be wonderful if every student came into the English classroom with the desire to write? If they only had the desire, we could help with the details. Unfortunately, they don't. And we can't expect all of them to. Although some will look forward to getting their thoughts on paper, others will dread it with a passion.

Our first task as English teachers is to help student writers see that the writing process can be enjoyable and has purpose. As teacher candidates, we felt that our teaching ability would be enhanced if we understood what goes on in the minds of student writers. We wanted to find out what makes the avid writer tick and what prevents the reluctant writer from fluency. We conducted this study through one-on-one interviews with our students.

CONDUCTING INTERVIEWS

The first step of our research was to find out *who* these writers were. Our mentor teachers helped us select one student who was a consistently avid writer and one whom they considered a consistently reluctant writer. Some of us asked for a show of hands of students who would be willing to volunteer for our study, after we explained the purpose of our research. Next, we set up 15-minute interviews with each student to discuss his or her feelings about writing. Most of us found that our students were more than willing to talk to us privately about their writing habits. They enjoyed the attention, and we benefited from the opportunity of getting to know these students on a deeper level.

The interviewing styles and techniques were as wide and varied as our own assortment of personalities, but the format was designed to put the student at ease. Some of us felt more comfortable writing down a detailed list of questions; others of us dove right in and let the interview develop its own course. We started by asking a simple question, such as, "How do you feel about writing?" Our more talkative students led us into engaging, lively discussions, while our more timid ones waited for our prodding. At the very least, we established genuine student–teacher rapport.

Earlier in the year, we had been asked to write our own writer's autobiography, which taught us how to explore our feelings about writing. So we asked the students the same types of questions, such as:

- Do you like to write? Why or why not?
- What is your favorite type of writing? Least favorite?
- Have you ever had a teacher inspire you? Discourage you? Describe how he or she made you feel.
- Do you remember a time when you really began to like to write?
- Do you remember a time when you stopped liking to write?
- Do you keep a journal or do any kind of writing at home?
- What do you think teachers can do to make writing more fun?

COMPARING STUDENT VOICES

After the interviews, each teacher candidate wrote a first-person narrative to share with the rest of the class. One at a time, we read a case out loud. Without comment, we then read the next one (see Hudson-Ross, Miller-Cleary, & Casey, 1991). Soon, the voices of 20 avid writers and 20 reluctant writers filled the room. As we listened to each other, we immediately began to see patterns emerging. It was not difficult to recognize that certain trends exist within and across each group of student writers (see Figure 7.1). We took note of these trends, and we began to see that our challenge as future teachers would be to develop lesson plans that ultimately would meet these students' needs.

Figure 7.1. Student writer trends.

Avid Writers	Resistant Writers
• Keep journals	• View writing as hard
• Parent encouragement	• Dislike assigned topics
• Good self-perception	• Nothing to say
• Need topic to work with	• Grammar/mechanics errors
• Have purpose	• No time
• Organized	• Teacher discouragement
• First drafts	• Bored
• Like school writing	• Computers make writing fun
• Make outlines	• Writing is too long
• Favored teacher influence	• No patience
• Use computers	• Don't like own writing
• Write day before due	• No rough draft
• Relate to books	• Can't express self
• Like independent projects	• Music/background noise helps
• Read past writings	• Poor spelling
• Like teacher guidelines	• Despise red ink (bloody paper)
• Like teacher response	• Sad/angry when writing
• Write to God	• Organizational problems
• Enter contests	• Do it for grade
• Overachiever	• Can't remember details
• Like feedback from others	• Write music on own
• Write to relieve fear	• Self-conscious
• Write for other classes	• Hate free-writing
• Worried about grammar	• Too many rules
• Take advanced English	• Too busy
• Hate red ink	
• Enjoy poems and short stories	
• Inspired	
• Real-life writing	
• Love to read	
• A/B students	
• Personal writing	

Avid Writers

Regardless of school or tracking level, we found several common response trends from students who enjoy writing. One is that students prefer a personal response to their writing versus the red ink that slashes through not only their words but also their self-esteem. While there is certainly a time and place for correcting student errors, students thrive on positive feedback. One of the mentor teachers in our field center takes the time to type personal comments for each student paper. Susan, a student in this teacher's class, says she prefers this personal response because "it lets me know what people feel when they read my work."

Avid writers also enjoy reader response. Megan, a first-year high school student who wrote a short story for a class assignment, was encouraged by written responses from her peers:

> I wrote this story about a girl who's flashing back after she died of AIDS. I got such positive feedback from it, I was encouraged to write more like it. Everyone said it was very powerful, so I've thought about getting it published. I was really surprised at the way things turned out.

Predominantly, avid student writers admit writing poetry as an outlet for their feelings. Brandy, a junior, said that she likes writing poetry because it is creative and has no set structure, so she enjoys "writing poetry on [her] own." Susan responded with, "I write mostly poems, sometimes letters and journals. You can just say what you feel; you don't have to worry about plot or anything like that."

Several enthusiastic student writers indicated having a structured writing process. Cedrick, a senior, explained the difference between writing at school and at home:

> In class, I go through a typical process of writing the five-paragraph essay. It helps you organize your thoughts, think about it, and jot down what is important and needs to be said. I try to get to the direct and indirect meanings. The in-class writing is based on organizing thoughts, and you may like that or you may not. Outside of class, I write when my emotions are stirred up . . . with no format. This is my best writing.

Another common trend among students who enjoy writing is they feel support from their family, teachers, or peers. Susan shared, "People that have read things I have written have encouraged me to write." Megan mentioned an experience where a teacher made her feel like she had talent in writing. "I remember the last day of school in the eighth grade when my teacher gave back a story I wrote about my grandfather. She said it was beautiful and that it was the best of the whole lot." Two years later, Megan attributes her success in writing to this teacher's encouragement.

Reluctant Writers

Our students gave many different reasons for not liking to write, the most common being that they see writing as a difficult process. The students find writing laborious enough to avoid doing the work altogether, or they approach it haphazardly. One student came right out and said, "I ain't afraid to write, I just hate it."

Many of the students mentioned boredom as a reason they don't like to write. David said, "Writing is boring and takes up time. I'd rather be playing golf." Another student said, "I don't like writing school stuff, but I like writing letters and about softball and cheerleading." Reluctant writers shared that their lack of interest in the assignment often made the writing process a chore. Some students mentioned having no patience or that the classroom atmosphere was too noisy or distracting. Others felt they had organizational problems or trouble remembering details. One student felt that she could not write because she always started getting off the subject, and she didn't know how to organize. Therefore, she said, she always got a bad grade anyway.

The most common complaint students expressed was how they hate receiving papers back that have red ink all over them. Mechanics seem to be a recurring enemy among first-year high school students. Stuart said that his ninth-grade teacher destroyed his confidence:

> She was too picky about everything, and finally I stopped liking to write. If I missed one comma or something, the whole paper was wrong. I never had spelling problems; it was the little mistakes like fragments and commas that got me. There are too many rules. [She] really turned me off of [writing] with the way she graded.

Resistant writers repeatedly said that they had trouble expressing themselves or were self-conscious about their writing. They also mentioned having poor handwriting skills. One student said his hand always gets tired from writing. Others mentioned that they dislike writing by hand but enjoy writing by computer.

Before we interviewed these students, we never realized how much diversity would be expressed in their reluctance to write. Their sincere, realistic answers made us realize that asking a student one-on-one about how he or she feels about writing can make a difference in that student's educational experience in our classroom.

REFLECTING ON OUR RESEARCH

Through conducting these writing interviews, we discovered many things about our students and realized how useful the experience was for ourselves and the students involved. We found out who likes to write and who doesn't; what topics students like to write about and those they despise; where they enjoy writing and under what conditions; and how they feel about input they receive on their writing.

From this information that we learned about individual students, we are more capable of incorporating their interests into writing activities. One teacher candidate learned that her student, Thomas, likes to write comics and keeps dream logs at home, but he doesn't enjoy writing at school. Thomas told her:

> I started writing because I wanted to make a comic book series. When I write, I like writing at home. I have, like, this meditation I do—Narcaina. I mostly write about dreams. I get my stories from dreams. When I write outside school, I don't worry about correctness. I like writing at night . . . when a full moon approaches. Like, I just woke up or something, and things come to me. This is when I write the most.

Although Thomas may not enjoy formal writing in school, this teacher candidate now knows the importance of using activities that will meet his artistic needs. This is true for many who have other intelligences in our classrooms, but lack strong formal linguistic abilities (Gardner, 1993).

Another teacher candidate said his interview with a student helped him get to know her more personally:

> Jill is probably the quietest girl in the advanced classes I have, but I was surprised when a couple of weeks ago she came up to me after class and asked me about writing. . . . This quiet girl actually had a great deal to say and, besides being a writer, she is also an accomplished piano and violin player.

Our teacher research not only helped us better understand the personalities and needs of our students, but we also learned about ourselves and reflected on our educational backgrounds. Many of us remember teachers we liked, who encouraged us in our writing so that now we want to teach the subject. We also remember those who hindered our progress as writers. After doing our own writer autobiographies, we can see a connection between ourselves and our students as writers.

One teacher candidate said she suddenly realized that she was grading student papers in a way that discourages student writers:

> Not too long after these interviews, my mentor teacher gave me back a set of essays that I had previously graded. She told me that I needed to grade them again. Guess what I had done? I had destroyed the essays with red ink and made no positive comments. I was shocked! I couldn't believe that I was one of *those* teachers.

All of us realize we will be more conscious of our grading efforts, seeking to write encouraging responses.

BEYOND THE CLASSROOM

Another positive outcome of our research is that we feel that we were able to encourage the good writers to write even more, to push themselves, and to strive to reach new goals. Megan, after having read her short story to the teacher candidate conducting the interview, was encouraged to enter it in a *Seventeen* Magazine fiction writing contest. She got the application that very day.

Several avid writers mentioned a parent or another adult in their personal lives who had encouraged them to read for pleasure and to write. One student's mother had written a mystery novel that she had never sent to a publisher, and the student positively beamed as she told about her mother's ability. As teachers, we can create assignments and activities that involve these adults, such as having this student's mother come read an excerpt from her book in class and give tips on how to write a mystery plot or overcome writer's block.

Beth Tatum, a mentor teacher in the program, asks students to read a book on their own and choose an adult to read the same book (Tatum, 1997). After reading the book, the student and adult hold a discussion about the book, recording it on tape or writing about it afterwards. This teacher says the interaction between students and adults about reading and writing is priceless; in the process, both learn about each other and real communication takes place.

Through our research, we've learned what really matters when it comes to teaching student writers—instilling them with purpose. Rusty, a senior, describes what he feels is important about writing:

> I feel that the purpose of writing is to express how humans feel, to interact with others, to express point of view on life. Most people write because something is on their minds. They can write without taking it out on others. I want to make a statement with my writing.

We can't argue with a statement like that!

REFERENCES

Gardner, H. (1993). *Multiple intelligences: The theory in practice.* New York: Basic Books.

Hudson-Ross, S., Miller-Cleary, L., & Casey, M. (1991). *Children's voices.* Portsmouth, NH: Heinemann.

Tatum, B. (1997). Capturing authentic conversations about literature. *Connections, 34*(1), 3–15.

CHAPTER 8

Small Group Book Sharing in Secondary Schools:
A Teacher Candidate Research Project

Jennifer McDuffie Stewart & Peg Graham

*Teacher candidate Jennifer McDuffie Stewart extended her research into stu-
dent reading habits and preferences by implementing a book sharing project in
her high school English class. Here, Jennifer and Peg tell the story of what unfolded from Jennifer's perspective as she closely observed her students' reactions
to choosing their own books and talking with classmates about their reading.
Although Jennifer answered some of her questions about students as readers
with this project, she continues to reflect on her initial concerns about school-
sponsored reading. In the retrospective at the end of the chapter, Jennifer—now
a second-year teacher at Habersham Central High School in Mount Airy, Georgia—explains her current thinking on the topic.*

It took me about 3 weeks at Oconee County High School to receive my first
big shock as a student teacher: My students did not like to read! Every time
a reading assignment was made, I observed the pained expressions on their
faces and heard a chorus of groans. I was honestly stunned by this little
discovery. I had always loved to read, and found it hard to grasp the idea
that some of these teenagers possibly had never read a book cover to cover.

After struggling with this foreign notion for a few days, I decided that it
was time to start looking at the problem realistically. I had to temporarily
forget about my own reading habits and look closely at the habits and preferences my students had developed as readers. I knew that if I was ever going
to help them cultivate a love of reading and a knowledge of books, first I
needed to learn what they were already capable of and interested in doing. I
wanted to know who liked to read, what their favorite books were, why some
students did not like to read, which authors they had been exposed to, and

other information that would give me a better understanding of what I was facing as their English teacher.

At about this time, we were beginning to think about possible topics for our research projects in my class at the University of Georgia. I made a list of ideas I was interested in and realized that I kept coming back to these questions about the students' reading habits. I wondered if I could create some sort of project that would provide me with concrete answers, insights that would be helpful once I was on my own in the classroom. I already knew that just placing novel after novel in a student's hands in hopes that one would catch her attention and turn her into a reader for life was not likely to work.

I decided to share my concerns with my university colleagues and get some feedback. I did not have any specifics about an alternative, but my ideas were beginning to fit together and carry my thinking in a new direction. In my journal I described what I thought was the problem and listed the questions I wanted to answer. As I brought the entry to a close, I added a concluding sentence and then reread what I had written. Any previous doubts dissolved. Without even really thinking about it, I had summed up the thought that had been tugging at the back of my mind since the first week of school: "The books that I think are so exciting mean absolutely nothing to some students." Seeing my words on paper made me realize how important they were. I could not influence students to become readers until I understood why they were not readers in the first place. The encouraging comments from one of my professors, Sally Hudson-Ross, gave me the final boost of confidence I needed before finalizing my ideas and proceeding with a project I hoped would teach me more about my students as readers and motivate them to read more.

DESIGNING THE RESEARCH PROJECT

I decided that I wanted to try the individualized reading project we were doing in our university class with the tenth-grade class I had at Oconee. I was familiar with how it worked and had really enjoyed participating in it. This simple project involved reading a book, making a "footprint" out of construction paper, writing a recommendation for the book on the "footprint," sharing the book with a small group, and displaying the "footprint" around the room for others to read. As I began to work out the details for my official research proposal, I realized that the project was going to teach me as much about teaching as about my students' reading habits. For the first time, I had to figure out how to prepare a successful lesson. I initially planned for the students to read one book a week, as we did in our university class, but recommendations from my classmates made me question whether this was a realistic expectation. I had not had to consider work loads before, and it was a tough issue to deal with. I knew from my experience that if I assigned too many books, students most likely would become discouraged and stop reading them. Afraid this would happen, I decided that one book every other week would be fine. I realized that assigning books would always be difficult, knowing that students read at different paces and in different circumstances. I also realized that I would have to remember that each student in my class had five other subjects to study for.

My next dilemma also was brought to my attention by my classmates. How could I make sure that the students were reading (and completing) the books they chose? This is still a problem I have not solved. For my research, I created a list of projects that could accompany any book and decided that students would complete one for every book they read, in addition to their "footprint" recommendations. I was not completely satisfied with this because I wanted the emphasis to be on reading, not on the project that was being handed in and graded. I knew that if I was ever to try this reading project on a larger scale, I would have to create another form of evaluation that would make completing the novel the final goal.

STUDENT REACTION

I created a packet describing the individualized reading project for my students and became more and more excited about how it would work. I felt that I had improved my proposal and that I was more than ready to present it to the class. Unfortunately, once I did so, the students were not quite as thrilled about the project as I was. A look of disgust gleamed in every eye. I must admit, I was extremely disappointed. I had put so much work into this assignment, but they were far from appreciative!

It was clear that even though the students were being offered choices about what they could read, they were unenthusiastic. That made me feel even more strongly that reading had become a mere school chore to these teenagers. They viewed it as work, not as a chance to choose their own books, experiment with new authors, or get input and recommendations from peers.

As I wrote in my journal on that first day, I was frustrated and let down, but when I reviewed that entry later, I began to think the situation was not as bad as I first had thought. The students responded negatively to my project idea, an idea based on my hypothesis that allowing students to choose their own books and discuss them with friends would create better readers. However, in the questionnaires they filled out on the first day, a majority of students told me that "[they] wish [they] could choose books on [their] own, and that [they] could read a book that was recommended by a friend." In order to explain this contradiction to myself, I chose to believe that what the students wrote on the questionnaires were their true feelings, and their reactions in class resulted from the idea of being assigned more homework in general. I decided that once the class adjusted to the reading schedule, I would be able to get more honest reactions.

By the second week, I began to think that the project was going to work out after all. I had allowed students to choose a book on their own and, I must admit, I was skeptical about the quality of the books they would choose. I worried that they would select short books rather than interesting books. I had no reason to worry. Students chose novels that would impress any English teacher. I noticed that these 15- and 16-year-old students were much more interested in reading classics and best sellers than the adolescent fiction I had been learning about in my university class. They seemed to view these young adult books as childish.

That same week, I realized that I had learned two more important tips for encouraging reading. Because of the censorship controversy in my school, I had tried to play it safe by limiting students to the books found in the school library. I noticed that this immediately made the students feel restricted, and they pointed out that the school library did not have copies of the new books they wanted to read. I knew they were right. I had tried to encourage them to experiment, but at the same time had unintentionally put limitations on their choices. I realized how important this sense of freedom was when I mentioned that they could choose a novel they had read before. This small allowance seemed to please several of them. Initially I was planning to encourage them to choose different books, but then I thought about how often I read some of the same books over and over again. This is one aspect of reading that I plan to remember.

PROJECT OUTCOMES

As the biweekly sessions of this 12-week project flew by, some really exciting things unfolded. Students began to feel more comfortable discussing their novels with their small groups, often actually forcing me to end their conversations because time was up. Each group was allowed to choose one "Book of the Week" to present to the entire class. This evolved from my initially begging a student to share his book title and a *brief* summary, to students volunteering to go to the podium and "selling" to their classmates what they thought was a great book.

Even more exciting was that the same books began to pop up in different groups each session, which meant that they were beginning to take suggestions and recommendations from each other, branching out from the kinds of books they usually chose. As one student said, "Now I think I can start to read other books besides ones about Star Trek."

My true feeling of accomplishment finally came during the fifth session. I made an announcement to the class that since exams were coming up the following week, I was going to cancel the final book share. I expected cheers and sighs of relief. The students had been filling out reading journals every other week, and I knew that many of them saw the project simply as extra work. However, instead I heard comments like, "But I already read my book for next week," and "I already picked the book I want to read." My second major shock as a student teacher: *These students were actually enjoying the assignment.* I was more than willing to hold another book share. To take some of the pressure off, I told them that they could just read a book and discuss it, instead of completing one of the small projects to accompany it. This worked out well, especially since that had been my original plan.

EVALUATING THE PROJECT/STUDENT FEEDBACK

There were a lot of positive comments on the final questionnaires. One student explained how she had changed as a reader: "I used to shy away from deeper, more thought-provoking books and stuck to novels that did nothing to enhance my vocabulary or views whatsoever. Now I dive into things like this with no hesitation at all." Several students thought they had become faster readers, and also better at understanding story lines.

The majority of the students liked the chance to participate in the small group book shares. While some simply enjoyed being able to have a discussion about a book they had read, others felt that summarizing their book out loud actually improved their understanding. They seemed to want to make their book sound interesting to classmates, so they remembered all of the details they could.

Finally, what I see as the best part of this project, was allowing students to choose their own books. This was viewed by the students, even those who did not like the project at all, as a positive aspect. One student suggested that "the number one reason typical teens don't enjoy reading is because they are forced to read books they don't enjoy." Another said, "I liked being able to read a book without a teacher breathing down my back and giving me tests about its contents. That makes you hate the book." One suggestion I did get, though, was, "It would be cool if you gave a book list of recommended books. That would probably 'broaden our horizons.'" I think this is definitely something I will do next time I try this project. Book recommendations from classmates helped some students make selections, but I do not want to neglect the student who wrote, "I wandered through the library aimlessly not knowing what I could experience if I only plucked a book off the shelf and read it."

While this project seemed to go over well with the majority of the class, I do not want to imply that every student loved it. Several students who said they liked to read, strongly resented being told when to do it. The students in this class were also very grade-oriented, and many of them saw this project as just that—a school project. It "interfered." One student wrote that her goal was "to not let my reading interfere with my study time." Because the books they read were not being studied in class or covered on a test, some students did not value the experience. At least one student disliked the project so much that he established as his reading goal for the remainder of the year "not to read another novel for my English class if I can help it."

However, I feel that overall the project was a success. My next goal is to find a way to make this work with my own classes next year. I'm still learning the ropes, but when I hear a student say that an idea I developed "has gotten [her] to remember how much [she] enjoy[s] reading," I definitely feel that I am headed in the direction I want to be going. I am determined to introduce this type of independent reading to future classes.

REFLECTION: TWO YEARS LATER

As my second year of teaching draws to a close, I feel a sense of accomplishment mixed in with the assortment of emotions that take over during the last few weeks of the school year. I am still a beginning teacher, learning classroom management skills, trying to figure out cooperative learning, finding new and exciting ways to organize the chaotic room in which I spend so much of my time. However, despite all of the confusion, I have stuck with the principles I had when I entered the profession. My students are reading.

During these 2 years, I have tried numerous approaches to reading. Book reports, presentations, essays, projects, anything I could think of, we tried. The results were tolerable. Some students read; some did not. No one was excited about his or her book. However, this last semester, I came full circle back to my small group book share idea. Initially, I had written off this idea. It had worked wonderfully during my student teaching, but I had attributed this to the fact that I tried it with one highly motivated class. I had plenty of time to keep track of the projects and readings. Unfortunately, I assumed that this idea would not work in a large, homogeneous ninth-grade class, which is what I would be teaching in my new position. I was wrong.

I made some changes in the original plan, but the crux of the idea, reading a book of choice and then discussing it, remained the same. To begin with, I gave my students a list of recommended books (I used the one listed in the appendix of *In the Middle* by Nancie Atwell, 1987). I had purchased various novels in sets of five for our English department. I gave mini-book talks for each of these and then offered students the opportunity to visit the school library or browse through our classroom collections if they were not interested in any of these. Finally, all students found something they were interested in reading.

To encourage the students to read in a relaxed, enjoyable manner, I explained that they would not be tested on the book. The looks of amazement made the entire project worthwhile for me! I told them they had 3 weeks to finish their books, unless they had chosen a very lengthy book, in which case we would work out an individual schedule. We read every day for the first 20 minutes of class (90-minute class periods made this possible). Each Friday, after reading, students were given time to write me a one- to two-page letter telling me about their books. I provided questions about plot, characters, likes/dislikes, predictions, and writing styles for students who needed guidance. At the end of the 3-week period, students brought in a "Book Block." This was a visual that was to be the size of one of the concrete blocks on the back wall of our classroom. On the block, students included the title, author, a brief plot summary, their opinion of the book, and a visual that would attract the interest of other potential readers. These blocks lined the wall so that any student searching for a new book had an immediate source of recommended reading. Finally, students met in small groups to discuss their books. The only requirement was that every person take a turn describing his or her reading experience.

The results of this project have been great. Students would sometimes beg for more time at the end of the 20 minutes. They traded books with each other and with me; they were actually excited about sharing their experience with someone else. Of course, as always, there are still aspects to be improved. As I suspected, keeping up with 60 students is difficult. When I try this again next year, I will need to find a more organized system for sorting out the letters I receive and keeping track of what individual students are reading at a given moment. Responding to student letters also proved to be difficult and time-consuming. Next time I may try having students alternate between writing me and writing a classmate. Furthermore, there were a handful of students who were still not interested in reading; some would pretend they had finished their book, while others would tell me honestly that they just didn't care. Some of these students could be nudged in the right direction; others never did catch on. I tried to keep it in perspective; after all, I knew that when students were assigned a common book to read at home, over half of the class usually did not finish the reading. It's hard to hold a student 100% accountable for reading when the goal is to read for enjoyment.

Overall, I feel that this idea is a success for readers in my classroom. The letters each week were a great way to maintain individual contact during the busy semester. Many students would begin a new book as soon as they finished the one they were reading. A sophomore in the class, who previously had failed ninth-grade English, said, "I used to hate this [reading]. Now I feel kind of funny if I don't have a book to read." Now *I* remember why I wanted to teach.

REFERENCE

Atwell, N. (1987). *In the middle: Writing, reading, and learning with adolescents.* Portsmouth, NH: Boynton/Cook.

CHAPTER 9

Using a Behavior Journal to Discover What Causes Disruptions: A Teacher Candidate Research Project

Jeff Anderson

Jeff and his mentor teacher, Fran Bullock, launched into a collaborative effort to find out more about how to engage their ninth-grade students. One of the tools they found useful was the behavior journal, which provided them with a strategy for recording how students responded to particular classroom activities and teacher behaviors. As Jeff explains here, he has discovered that some behavior patterns are relatively consistent regardless of the classroom context.

Anyone who has ever taught high school—especially to students who experience limited school success—knows that behavior is an enormous issue. In my limited experience as a teacher, my biggest frustrations stem from behavior problems in my classroom. I probably spend as much, if not more, time thinking of ways to control behavior as I do deciding how to teach the curriculum. Classroom management was a great concern of mine when I began student teaching, and it still is today. In fact, it was that concern that led me to keep a behavior journal as part of my collaborative research project with my mentor teacher.

CHOOSING A COLLABORATIVE INQUIRY PROJECT

Before I delve too deeply into behavior journals, some background information on my collaborative research project is in order. My mentor teacher and I conducted research in three of our classes (all ninth-grade students) from October until February, when I presented our work at the Georgia Council of Teachers of English (GCTE) conference in Savannah. The focus of our research was how to motivate these students. A portion of that research involved answering the following questions:

- What impact does classroom management have on student motivation?
- What types of classroom activities lead to the least/greatest amount of off-task behavior?

In order to answer these questions, I began keeping a behavior journal.

PURPOSE OF THE BEHAVIOR JOURNAL

The significance of the name "behavior journal" cannot be overlooked. More specifically, the word *behavior* cannot be overlooked. As an English teacher, I like to use dictionaries, so I consulted *Webster's College Dictionary* (1st ed.) for help in defining this term. I found the following definition of "behavior" to be most appropriate: "the action or reaction of any material under given circumstances." Accordingly, my behavior journal was a record of the actions or reactions of students under given circumstances. In particular, I was interested in the circumstances that I as a teacher could influence.

Obviously, some circumstances are beyond the teacher's control. The teacher cannot dictate how a student might feel on a particular day. The teacher has no control over a student's home life. The teacher is limited to a certain extent by the physical parameters of his or her classroom. With the behavior journal, my aim was simply to observe, so that I could determine what could and could not be controlled within a classroom. I wanted to find out which activities led to student engagement and which activities caused students to be most disruptive. So, while my mentor teacher taught, I observed. Everything she did I wrote down. Everything the students did in response I also wrote down. She and everything she did were "given circumstances," and the students were "materials." Their resulting behavior, as the definition states, was the "action" or "reaction" to what she did. In order to determine how much of this behavior could be controlled, all of the factors involved had to be analyzed.

FINDINGS FROM THE BEHAVIOR JOURNAL

After compiling my behavior journal (which spanned the months from October to February), I read through it, searching for patterns of on- and off-task behavior. Having done so, I compiled a list of those patterns. As I look back on that list in retrospect—after having taught full time for a year—I come to an important realization: Two different groups of students are not as likely to be engaged by the same activities as they are to be disengaged by the same activities.

To comprehend this realization, consider first my teaching background. I currently teach English to ninth graders. They are quite similar to the ninth-grade students I taught during my teacher candidate duty. In fact, the reading and writing skills of both groups are comparable.

You may be wondering what a comparison of my two teaching experiences has to do with my behavior journal. When I compiled the research that I did during my teacher candidate experience for the purpose of presentation at the GCTE conference, I made the following statements regarding the behavior journal:

> I am not attempting to make generalizations about what activities will be successful in all classroom situations; however, these patterns were fairly consistent in three general classes, so they arguably could be transferable to other situations.

I feel that these statements merit some consideration. In fact, this is where my experience in my current teaching position becomes relevant. Now that I have had the opportunity to work in a school other than the one where I student taught, with students other than those particular ninth graders, I feel that I am in a better position to argue whether those behavior patterns are indeed "transferable."

BEHAVIOR PATTERNS ACROSS TWO SCHOOLS

I will begin by discussing the patterns of on-task behavior that I noted in my behavior journal during my student teaching year. On February 6, 1995, I recorded in my behavior journal the responses of my three ninth-grade classes to the same assignment. My mentor teacher placed paper plates of different sizes and designs on the chalk tray. She then asked the students to write a journal entry in which they were to give the paper plates human characteristics. The journal writing served as an introduction to a lesson on personification and the poem "The Legend of the Paper Plates" by John Haines. Consider the behavior of each class, as noted in my behavior journal, after having been given the assignment:

Second period

Everyone writing but Marie. Garrett walks in late, asks someone what's going on. Keith and Carlos (sitting near Garrett) are laughing. Kade, Gary, and Trisha are writing diligently. Gary asks, "Are you gonna put us in our seating chart today?" Garrett asks, "Do I need to make up work from Friday?"

Fourth period

A few comments, then complete silence. Mike asks a question, Fran answers.

Fifth period

Students quiet. David has nothing on his desk—Fran walks over to him; he gets out paper and writes. Josh whistling "Andy Griffith"—disrupts several students who tell him to be quiet.

For the most part, the majority of students in all three classes were engaged by this particular journal entry. The off-task behavior in second period seemed to result from a student coming in late, not the assignment. In fifth period, a student who engaged in off-task behavior was reprimanded quickly by his peers. All of the behavior in fourth period was positive and related to the task at hand. Overall, the activity brought about a desirable result from my students. This pattern of on-task behavior also was evident on several other occasions when I observed those students writing journal entries. Moreover, I found journal writing to work extremely well with the ninth graders I taught in my own classroom. In fact, my students usually wrote in their journals for slightly longer periods of time without becoming disruptive than did those students I taught during my student teaching.

A number of other activities that led my students to be most engaged during my field experience year met with similar response from the students at my current school. Tests, for example, almost always engaged both groups of students for long periods of time. Groupwork in which students had to complete an exercise usually brought about desirable behavior from the students at both schools. In terms of student behavior, free reading time was generally a success at both schools. Other situations that led to patterns of on-task behavior at both schools include the following: when the teacher asked follow-up questions in response to student questions; when specific instructions were given for what to do upon completion of an in-class assignment; and when the teacher and students worked through an assignment together in a discussion format.

On the other hand, I have tried several activities with my current classes—activities that engaged my former students—and had minimal success. Moreover, some of the activities that worked well in my student teaching year led to disruptive behavior in my first year of full-time teaching. For example, students in my student teaching year responded well when asked to share journal entries, but the students I taught my first year of teaching generally resisted the same activity. In addition, my former students often paid attention and asked relevant questions when instructions were being given at the beginning of an assignment. However, during my first year of teaching, my students often became disruptive or did not listen when initial instructions were being given. Many of them had a tendency to interrupt with irrelevant questions or statements. These contrasting behaviors between the two groups of students lead me to the following conclusion: The patterns of on-task behavior noted in my behavior journal during my student teaching year are not necessarily transferable to all classroom situations.

However, when I look at the patterns of *off-task* behavior that I noted in my behavior journal, it is a different story altogether. Without a doubt, the patterns are transferable to my current students. Almost all of the activities that led my former students to be disruptive had the same effect on my current students. Listed below are just a few of the classroom situations that as a rule caused students to be disruptive in my student teaching classes:

- Near the end of an assignment.
- When a student asks an irrelevant question or makes an irrelevant comment
- Taking care of school business (e.g., role, having a new student sign for a book, new seating chart)
- Asking a student in front of other students if he or she brought the proper materials to class
- When the intercom comes on
- If the desks are rearranged when a "floating" teacher gets to the room
- When a book drops on the floor
- When a student who doesn't read well is reading aloud
- When the door is open
- When the teacher talks for several minutes without eliciting comments from students
- If the teacher looks at the clock while talking to students
- Near the end of the period
- After being in groups for an extended period of time
- When the teacher is sitting at a desk
- When some students are still working on an assignment, but most have finished and have nothing to do
- When a student walks in late

These situations always caused my students to indulge in off-task behavior. Interestingly, when I reflect on my first year at my current school, I can remember specific instances of every single one of these situations leading to off-task behavior. (The list is excerpted from the compilation of behavior patterns included in my research project. It is based on my behavior journal.)

IMPLICATIONS FOR TEACHING

Keeping in mind that my comparisons involve students at only two different schools, an interesting conclusion perhaps can be drawn. Based on the patterns noted in my journal and my own personal observations, it would appear that the same types of activities will always foster a disruptive environment in the classroom. On the other hand, activities that may work in one classroom may not work in another.

How can this information be put to practical use? My advice to student teachers: Observe other teachers. When you do, keep a behavior journal. However, limit what you record in the journal to disruptive situations. Make notes of the actions and/or activities that led to those disruptions. Start thinking about what you can do to avoid those same disruptions in your classroom. Develop procedures for handling those types of situations before they occur or, if at all possible, think of ways to eliminate those situations altogether. If possible, get someone, maybe a mentor teacher, to keep a behavior journal while you teach. A behavior journal will not solve all of your "first-year" classroom management problems, but it will help you to develop a plan. And I know a certain teacher who needed all the plans he could get during that first year!

CHAPTER 10

The Research Team: A Project Involving Mentor Teacher, Teacher Candidate, and Their Students

Christina Healan & Amy Wilbourne

From the beginning of their research project, Christina, a mentor teacher, and Amy, her teacher candidate, shared equal roles. They chose the topic together, and they distributed the data collection duties equally. They took turns as teacher and as researcher, providing a depth to their shared classroom work that one teacher alone could not achieve. As their project expanded, they involved their students in applied communications classes in data collection and analysis. They truly worked as a team and achieved benefits for all. This is the story of their work, told in alternating voices.

CHOOSING A TOPIC

Christina: I wanted to choose a project that would benefit me, Amy, and the students. I realized that we had to give careful consideration to our research topic and its possible outcomes. I also understood that our topic had to be realistic and not too broad. Because I had more experience and was much more familiar with the students and their needs, it was very important for me to be involved in helping to choose the topic. I was teaching a new and innovative Tech Prep class called Applied Communications, and Amy expressed an interest in learning more about this particular classroom. Applied Communications is a curriculum where vocational skills are integrated into the academic English classroom. To be in the Applied Communications class, students had to be within the top 50 percentile on their basic skills in reading comprehension and writing on the Iowa Test of Basic Skills. The focus of this course is to give non-college-bound students the motivation to learn in their academic subjects. Many of the traditional aspects of regular English classes are still a part of Applied Communications courses (reading and responding to literature, writing, speaking); however, there is an added vocational component as well as a focus on incorporating the communication skills of a typical language arts classroom with the needs of the vocational world. Since Tech Prep is a part of almost every school in the state of Georgia, I felt that Amy could benefit from researching the program—and I would benefit as well. I had taught Applied Communications for 2 years, but I often wondered about the effectiveness of the program. This project would, hopefully, help validate my efforts and allow students to discover the importance of their work in the Applied Communications class. Up until our research, I had a hard time explaining to the students how the Applied Communications curriculum served them differently—and perhaps better—than the regular English classroom. The research we conducted was a learning experience for all three participants—mentor teacher, teacher candidate, and students.

Amy: I had never heard of Applied Communications until I met Christina. I knew nothing about Tech Prep and very little about vocational education. The Applied Communications classroom was a curiosity for me. I had learned a lot about the academic side of how to teach my subject, but I had never come across something as innovative as relating English to the world of work. I was fascinated and a bit skeptical. Did it really work? When Christina and I compiled a list of possible research topics, the Applied Communications classroom stood out. I relied on my mentor teacher's judgment because of her familiarity with the classroom and the students. I could see where the Applied Communications curriculum would consolidate our interest and sustain our enthusiasm. We chose to research motivational factors in the Applied Communications classroom to determine whether the Applied Communications curriculum was doing what it was supposed to do.

COLLECTING DATA

Christina: The second step in the research process was the data collection. Amy and I sat down and made some more lists. We had to decide what data we were going to collect, how we were going to collect them, and who was going to be responsible for each part.

We decided to collect quantitative and qualitative data about our students' motivation from a range of sources. We would collect numerical information on tardies, absences, completed assignments, and grade averages, and conduct interviews and surveys to seek the students' opinions about the Applied Communications class. We felt that we also needed to validate our findings with a control group. Our research would mean very little if we did not have anything to which we could compare it. Fortunately, I taught three regular curriculum English classes. We had to be very careful in our selection of the control group students in order to preserve the integrity of our findings. We had to find students in the regular English classroom whose test scores and percentile ranking matched the requirements for students enrolled in Applied Communications. It would not be fair to compare the results otherwise.

Amy: This is where the real work began for me. All of our school's records were in the county warehouse behind our school. It was like the warehouse scene in *Raiders of the Lost Ark*. There were hundreds of boxes stacked in hundreds of rows, and nobody knew where to find what I needed. They just told me to start looking. It was the middle of January, and the warehouse didn't have any heat! I was beginning to understand what it meant to make a sacrifice in the name of education. Eventually, I found the records. I then had to go through individual test scores. This was tedious work. However, it was fun to look at pictures of these high school students from when they were back in the first grade. It touched a place in my heart to see them so small and innocent. I had to restrain myself from looking at personal information within the folders. I did not think that I had a right to know more than what I had come to find. I went through all three class lists, approximately 90 students, and came up with only 15 students who would meet the class ranking requirements for the control group. As a result, I learned that a large percentage of the student population in our regular classes had test scores falling below average on their basic reading and writing skills, useful information for my later teaching. I also realized that we would have to reduce the number of subject students in the Applied Communications classroom from whom we would collect and compare data. Finally, we identified 15 students in Christina's Applied Communications class and 15 students in her regular English classes to participate in the research.

Christina handed me the statistical data on all of our chosen subjects. She collected these data from her student records, and then I compiled the information. I took my numerical information to the computer lab at the university and proceeded to learn how to use Microsoft Excel. I had never used a spreadsheet or made a graph on a computer before. I was a bit dismayed when I asked for help and was handed a 3-inch thick user's manual. I was determined to visually display our research, however, because I knew that it would be more convincing if I did. The computer did a fabulous job of bringing our data to life. As I plugged in the numbers, the graph showed that students in the Applied Communications classroom, as a whole, had fewer absences, tardies, and incomplete assignments. The average grade for the 15 students who were taking Applied Communication was 72.6. In contrast, the average grade for the 15 control group students in the traditional English class was 69.5. Our objective information began to suggest to us that the Applied Communications classroom really seemed to be working for our students.

I also collected a lot of subjective information from the research students through interviews and surveys. I asked them about the projects they did in their classrooms and what they enjoyed most about their English class. I had to learn how to ask a question in a way that would allow the student to elaborate his or her answer. I found that a brief general question was better than a long or too specific question. General questions gave them more room to answer. A large percentage of the Applied Communications classroom students felt their English class really related to the real world, believing that it was relevant and useful to their lives. Many of the regular English students described their class as boring and not important. Remember: Christina is the teacher for all of these students! Besides the learning value of the data, I also felt that the research project was helping me get to know the students and helping them get to know me. It was easier for me to remember names and faces after I had actually talked with a student. I found this instrumentally important when I began teaching.

Christina: It was not possible for me to collect a lot of data while I was in the process of teaching. Amy was available for pulling students from the classroom for interviewing and administering surveys; however, at this time, the students trusted me more than they did Amy. It was my role to explain the project to the students and discuss the benefits of the project with them. I assured them that the data collected would never be used against them and that their sincerity in their participation would have an incredible impact on future students. We also made sure to provide students with parental consent forms. The students were very enthusiastic about the project, and we had a 100% return on parental consent forms.

In addition to comparing absences, tardies, assignment completion, and grades, Amy and I wanted to compare students' communication skills, the major emphasis of our Applied Communications class. We chose 10 students from each group who were currently employed. With the permission of the students, I mailed an employer/employee survey to their employers. I included a cover letter, assuring the employers that their comments on the surveys would be kept confidential and that their honesty was very important to us. The results from these were quite interesting and were actually consistent with my assessment of students' classroom communication performances. After receiving the employer surveys about our students, we felt it was only fair to give the students an opportunity to express their views about their employers as well. Several students in the Applied Communications class coherently and competently explained problems with their employers' communication skills. I was thrilled: They were using what they had learned in the classroom in a working environment!

INVOLVING STUDENTS

Christina: In the collection of the data, I felt that it was very important for the students to have an active role. In the Applied Communications class, students were accustomed to filling out an evaluation after each unit. The evaluation gave them an opportunity to express their opinions on the value of the unit and to offer suggestions for improvements. All students had taken the evaluations seriously and offered some valuable suggestions.

For our research, Applied Communications students were invited to interview several peers who were in the regular classes about their attitudes toward English, literature, and writing. The Applied Communications students generated their own questionnaire, another job-related skill. After interviewing the other students, the Applied Communications students wrote a paragraph comparing and contrasting their own attitudes with those of the students they interviewed. Both sets of students shared some common feelings about English; however, in contrast to the regular English classroom students, the Applied Communications students felt that they understood the value and importance of being able to read, write, and speak fluently. This was another affirmation that Amy and I needed in order to determine the effectiveness of the Applied Communications classroom. We saw how students were motivated to learn when they understood the degree to which their academic performance might affect their futures.

CONTINUING TO EXAMINE DATA THROUGHOUT THE YEAR

Our data collection continued throughout the year. We used writers' notebooks (journals) to compare students' responses to literature topics. During a *Huckleberry Finn* unit, students in the Applied Communications class clearly responded to events of the novel on a higher level than the regular English students. They shared their opinions about Huck's inner conflicts and his struggle to do what was right when society told him he was wrong. They related how communication skills played an important role in Huck's and Jim's relationship, and how their similarities and differences obstructed and helped their understanding of each other. On the other hand, the regular classroom students had a difficult time getting beyond the basic concepts in the story.

Amy: My short story unit during spring quarter student teaching also proved to be much more successful with the Applied Communications students. Both classrooms had been given the same preparatory material before beginning their short story writing. They read several short stories, learned different writing techniques and styles, and learned the different parts of a short story.

In an extension of our research, I assigned the regular classroom students to write a short story individually, while I assigned the Applied Communications students to work in groups since collaboration is a major component of the course. The Applied Communications students—experienced working in groups—used their communication skills to produce a really good story. I assigned every member of the Applied Communications class a writing part in the short story: exposition, conflict, rising action, climax, falling action, or resolution. This way nobody shouldered any more responsibility than anyone else, and I could give an individual and a group grade. I also had each group select an editor, and I allowed the editor to assign different work tasks such as illustrations, typing, and editing to "assistants." Working together really seemed to empower the Applied Communications students.

In the meantime, the regular students, working individually, struggled. They reported feeling frustrated, bewildered, and overwhelmed. In the end, I read five really good short stories produced by the Applied Communications students and over 100 sometimes agonizingly bad stories produced by the regular classroom students. All of the Applied Communications students turned in their assignments, whereas 10 of my regular English classroom students did not bother to turn in anything at all. The Applied Communications way worked for me—in work load and enjoyment—as well as for the students.

EXAMINING THE PROJECT RESULTS

Benefits for the Teacher Candidate

Amy: I learned so many different things from our research. I learned the processes and the functions of a research project. I learned about the integration of vocational skills into the academic classroom. I learned how to conduct and teach an English classroom that is designed to meet the needs of students for our future job market. I learned techniques that I will use for my own future classrooms. I think I will always work in groups for short story writing. Overall, I am more well-rounded as a teacher because of the research experience and mindset I have gained.

I also learned about the students. I learned about their individuality and talents and gained insight into their perspectives on learning to read and write. I learned about the school and how to go about collecting and gathering information in such a large and complicated system. The research project gave me a real advantage when I started student teaching. I understood the new applied curriculum that I had to teach. I knew all of the students by name. We didn't have a lot of transition problems. They looked to me to answer questions and to help them with their work, just as they had Christina.

The research project also helped me gain the skills I needed to partici-pate professionally as an educator. I learned the importance of joining a professional organization. I was able to present our research at the Georgia Council of Teachers of English conference in Savannah. Christina and I also presented our research at the American Educational Research Association conference in San Francisco. What an opportunity! One individual even told us that they had learned more from our presentation than from any other presentation at the conference. It was a great feeling to have other profession-als interested in our research processes and findings.

Probably the most rewarding and enjoyable benefit of the research proj-ect was the relationship it helped me to establish with my mentor teacher. We had to work together from the beginning. We had to share ideas, thoughts, and feelings. We were not able to sit back and wait for a long period of time before we actually had to communicate. As the research project progressed, so did our friendship. Going to San Francisco together really brought us together on a personal level. We were able to share the success and the re-wards of our hard work and simply enjoy each other's company without the demands of a hectic school day. I learned that Christina did wear blue jeans and tennis shoes and that she was adventurous and energetic, too.

Benefits for the Mentor Teacher

Christina: Besides affirmation of the effectiveness of the applied classroom, I was also encouraged greatly by the comments and the suggestions of all the students involved in the project. Their willingness to participate was very uplifting. Sometimes, I feel as if I am talking to robots or brick walls. Through a research mindset, however, I began to see that some students really do care about the quality of the education they are receiving. After examining the data collected, I began to see numerous benefits for students taking the Applied Communications course, but I also realized that the regu-lar English course could be strengthened to meet more of the needs of all students. The students who have chosen not to take the Applied Communi-cations class have good reasons, for the most part. To take the Applied Com-munications course, they must enjoy working with others, and some students just prefer to work alone. There is no reason, however, that this curriculum cannot be used to address some job and communication skills in the regu-lar classroom.

The most important benefit for me has been the opportunity to get to know my students well. Although our intense observation and collaboration with them made it much more difficult to give them up at the end of the year, I knew so much more about this group of students than any other group I had taught previously. I really believe the old cliché that teachers touch lives forever. For the first time, I felt I had touched their lives, and they definitely had touched mine.

Benefits for the Students

Amy: The transition time when the teacher candidate takes over the classroom may be a difficult experience for him or her, but it also can be very trying for the students. Many times, students feel betrayed by their "real teacher" and confused about the stranger trying to replace her. I felt the research project smoothed the transition for our students and me. I was not a stranger in this classroom. When I assumed primary teaching responsibility for classes, I knew that the students missed Christina, but they did not treat me as though I was invading their turf. They accepted me, and many went out of their way to make me feel comfortable.

The students were also well aware of the fact that Christina and I had a good relationship. They knew that Christina trusted me to collect information she valued, and that made their trust in me come a little easier. Also, the students never questioned my role because they knew Christina and I were a team.

Our students also benefited from the research because they too were an active part of the research process. You could see many students swell with pride and importance as they answered interview questions. I believe that it was extremely important to them that we valued their opinions and considered those opinions in our decision making. A student who I thought was quiet and shy in the classroom was likely to open up and come alive in a one-on-one interview setting. Students need to feel good about themselves. The research project helped them do just that.

The students also benefited because I got to know them as individual people. I knew that Shane did not like to read or write, but I also knew that he was very good with his hands and enjoyed artwork. When assigning short story parts, I made sure that Shane was provided with artwork he could contribute for a grade. This did not excuse him from writing; it just allowed him a better chance to do something that motivated him and got him involved. I would never have thought to give him this opportunity had I not known more about him through our interview.

As I said at the beginning, I was not too sure whether the Applied Communications course was something I really believed in. After getting the results of our research, however, I was much more enthusiastic about the Applied Communications class. I felt motivated to design a career portfolio with the Applied Communications students, and I collected job information and materials for them. The students were very appreciative of my efforts.

I believe that future students will benefit from the insights into curriculum that Christina and I gained through our research effort. The research helped me believe in and understand the Applied Communications curriculum. It gave me the passion to teach a curriculum and utilize methods that will benefit my future students. I now know that what motivates many of the academically inclined students will not motivate many of the non-college-bound students. I have learned, however, that I can still teach both groups classical literature; I just have to do it in a different way. My research experience has made me a better teacher. It also has given me the opportunity to share my knowledge about the Applied Communications curriculum. By sharing what I know, I can help other teachers utilize principles of the applied curriculum in their own classrooms. I don't think there can be any greater satisfaction than inspiring a child to learn. Our research indicated that our Applied Communications students were indeed as inspired to learn as we were.

NOTE

Amy Wilbourne took her first public school job as a vocational coordinator at Russell Middle School in Winder, Georgia, a direct result of knowledge gained from her research project.

PART III

Issues of the Teacher Candidate

Like teacher candidates in any other educational setting, teacher candidates in our collaborative inquiry community are asked to struggle with difficult questions of theory and practice. Usually, the struggle takes place in isolation from the realities of students with names and faces and the challenge of real school schedules with deadlines and constraints unique to the educational profession. This part of our book honors that struggle and places the concerns of the teacher candidate at the forefront.

Think Pieces, one of the most important components of the university classroom setting, are thoroughly explained by teacher candidates in Chapter 11. These important writing experiences provide the impetus for classroom discussion among teacher candidates who have their concerns heard and responded to in multiple ways through the Think Piece process. Chapters 12 and 13 reveal teacher candidates struggling through instructional planning and teaching and through classroom management, respectively. In both of these important chapters, the teacher candidate authors speak openly of their fears of failing, their actual failures, and the learning processes that result from these challenging experiences.

On a very practical note, Chapters 14 and 15 provide specific advice regarding classroom discussions and routines. In Chapter 14 the teacher candidates take the reader through what they learned about creating the best environment for thought-provoking classroom discussions with their students, from deciding how many days to allow for discussion to determining the types of questions to ask students about literature. Chapter 15 includes tips the teacher candidate learned about confronting and conquering the clerical tasks demanded of teachers, by observing and emulating her mentor teacher and other teachers.

Again, all of these chapters and the ones preceding them provide practical advice and insight that can be appreciated by all members of our community—teacher candidates, mentor teachers, and university faculty. Carefully embedded in each of these chapters, however, is the evidence that these teacher candidates can and do wrestle with educational theory, reconciling it with their beliefs about the classroom, their own personal experiences as students, and their own practice as beginning teachers.

CHAPTER 11

Think Pieces: Connecting School and Campus Learning

Susanna Blackstone
with Erin McDermott, Gretchen King, Amy Ledvinka, &
Amy Ragland Ingalls

These authors from the graduating class of 1996 had the benefit of learning about Think Pieces from the previous class' experiences and products. Here, Susanna, Erin, Gretchen, Amy, and Amy explain their perspectives of how the Think Piece complemented their learning and growth as teachers and how their class devised criteria to help make the experience even more powerful. A sample Think Piece at the end shows how energetic the peer-to-peer exchange can become.

One of the greatest advantages to being a member of a cohort group is the opportunity to share ideas and suggestions with other students who are having many similar experiences. Instead of relying solely on class discussion, which often can be limited, our instructors created a method of incorporating a new type of interaction into our classroom routine by introducing us to the concept of the Think Piece. Often, in class discussion, a student experiences a variety of views; however, these views are rarely thought out or committed to any type of record. In addition, it is difficult to absorb 10 different viewpoints spoken at once. The Think Piece format avoids these concerns by providing us with an opportunity to share both reader's and writer's thoughts on paper.

THE THINK PIECE CONCEPT

A Think Piece is a weekly paper assignment, usually three to five pages long, which is actually an extended free-write on a topic that concerns us. Some weeks we were assigned a topic, such as reflecting upon texts that we had read or research we had completed. However, many times the topic was ours to choose, and we were able to write about whatever was on our minds at the moment.

Every Friday, we met as a class and shared our Think Pieces; our professors contributed one as well and participated in the process. We handed in our papers and received one in return to read, trading as we finished for a round-robin read/response period of an hour. As we read our classmates' Think Pieces, we wrote comments, questions, and suggestions directly onto the paper (see Figure 11.1). Our papers were returned covered with the heartfelt insights of our peers. We had the opportunity to read many different papers and receive many different viewpoints on our own submissions. We then opened up the class for an extended discussion of major issues, a special problem, or whatever emerged. Later, one of our professors also read every Think Piece and commented, and we shared the final piece with our mentor teachers.

The Think Piece served a variety of purposes for us as students. For example, it offered us an opportunity for intense self-reflection. Writing the Think Piece gave us the chance to go back over our experiences that week at school—in our changing lives from student to teacher or in our thoughts—and carefully examine the things that did and did not work. If we had a particularly bad experience one week, a Think Piece provided a chance to vent frustrations and get feedback or suggestions in order to learn from our perceived failures.

We probed deeply into our experiences, as both teachers and students, and shared those experiences with the class. Occasionally, this process was painful; however, it was also cathartic. We discussed our most distressing experiences and received helpful comments and suggestions from our classmates, many of whom were struggling through the same crises.

By sharing our Think Pieces with the rest of the class, we also built a sense of community and trust within our classroom. We realized we were all striving to overcome many of the same obstacles, and by sharing our insights these obstacles were overcome more easily. For example, one Friday four people wrote Think Pieces on the issue of classroom management, and another week several of us had concerns about grading and evaluating. We were able to commiserate with one another and also offer suggestions for the future.

In addition, we had the advantage of getting a variety of well-developed viewpoints. An hour allowed us enough time to make thoughtful comments on each paper. These written comments furnished a permanent record of our classmates' suggestions. These comments were further developed in the student-led discussion that followed our writing time. We had the chance to

Figure 11.1. Sample Think Piece.

DEALING WITH STUDENTS WHO HAVE SPECIAL NEEDS

By Jeff Anderson

Marginal comments from other teacher candidates, whose initials follow their comments:

During my student practicum, the following question arose in my mind: How does a teacher deal with a student that requires special, individual attention without slowing down the rest of the class? This question was not one that just popped into my head while I was standing in the classroom one day. It became a concern of mine due to an actual student in one of the ninth-grade general classes at Oconee County High School.

Fran Bullock (my cooperating teacher) and I first realized that this particular student might require special attention on the first day of school. On that day, the students in Mrs. Bullock's classes were asked to write about themselves. They also had an additional writing assignment. The aforementioned student turned in a sheet of paper explaining, in very poor English, that he was a Mexican and did not speak English very well. Apparently he did not understand the second part of the assignment, because he had not even started it. (Time was not an issue, because the students had more than enough time to complete both exercises.) Over the next few days, I noticed looks of confusion on this student's face when assignments were given. He would look around at his classmates' papers as though he was trying to figure out what to do. I saw him pull out a Spanish/English dictionary a couple of times. At the beginning of the second day of class, I went over to this student to make sure he understood the assignment. He was supposed to be writing about personal goals that he had set for himself for the year. I explained the assignment to him a second time—Mrs. Bullock had already gone over it once. After staring blankly at his paper for a few seconds, he then asked me how to spell the word *goal*. I told him and briefly defined the word for him. After that, I left him alone. He consulted his dictionary and eventually began to write.

In addition to not understanding assignments, this student has difficulty keeping up with class notes. For example, he was having a hard time following Mrs. Bullock when she was going over terms for the vocabulary section which they were required to keep in their notebooks. This vocabulary section is based on words the students encounter while reading. I noticed that this particular student failed to write down several of the terms and definitions. When Mrs. Bullock said the words, he appeared to be searching frantically in his text-

I'm curious about what steps have already been taken because it seems like it wouldn't take long before this student was completely lost.

—P.G.

How did he get this far?
—A.H.

(Cont.)

Figure 11.1 *(Cont.)*

book for anything that sounded like what she was saying.

I have voiced my concerns about this individual to Mrs. Bullock in our dialogue journal. However, I still wonder what a teacher can do to help a student such as this one. For one thing, a teacher cannot possibly be expected to watch a single student all the time or to repeat everything for that student. What frustrates me about his situation is that this student is capable of learning and is probably very bright; however, the language barrier is extremely difficult to overcome. When trying to help him, I am not sure how in depth I should explain things, because I do not know how much he understands. I do not want to insult his intelligence, but at the same time, I want him to know what's going on. I also wonder what a teacher's responsibility should be as far as this student goes. This student is, after all, in a ninth-grade high school English course. Should a teacher be required to teach someone how to speak English at this level? I would not think so. On the other hand, this is a student who needs help. If a teacher's ultimate goal is to reach every student in a classroom, then it would seem that every effort should be made to accommodate the needs of this particular individual in order to meet that goal.

> I was thinking that perhaps some concerted, concentrated effort should be made to figure out the proficiency level of this individual before any course of action is decided. Maybe a long one-on-one meeting?
>
> —S.N.

Deciding how to handle such a situation places a teacher in a dilemma. Spending too much time with one individual could be detrimental to the rest of the class. Spending too little time with an individual who needs the extra help is obviously going to negatively affect that student. It seems to me that the only alternative is to find some kind of middle ground. Perhaps the student whom I have spoken about needs to have his assignments written out for him. Of course, I don't exactly have a lot of experience teaching, so I don't know if this is asking too much out of a teacher or not. Writing the assignments on the board might help him (although Mrs. Bullock would have a hard time with that since she "floats" from room to room). The situation almost seems to call for an interpreter or at least someone who can speak Spanish fluently who could help this child. Maybe I am just underestimating his ability to speak English; whatever the case may be, his skills appear to be deficient in this area. Perhaps his placement in the English class will help him; I have wondered if this situation can be compared with the "least restrictive environment" issue which has led to the mainstreaming of students with disabilities into regular classrooms. On the other hand, I don't know how he can learn if he truly cannot understand the majority of what is being said. The fact is, this student *is* in this class, and he is the teacher's responsibility. But should he be treated just like

> Are there copies of the work available in his native language?
>
> —G.S.

> If this student's English is poor enough to completely lose him in class, would a completely separate syllabus be in order?
>
> —S.N.

> I am curious to know if you believe as I do that this student's goal should be to learn English—basic English—as opposed to the more complex level students will be trying to attain.
>
> —P.G.

(Cont.)

Figure 11.1 *(Cont.)*

the other students in the class? Or should he receive special treatment? I want to say that he should receive special treatment, for the following reason: He deserves the same right to education as his peers, and he should not be denied that right just because English is his second language. I have had Spanish courses in high school and college, but if I were sent to a Spanish-speaking country right now, I probably would not be able to keep up in even the most basic remedial class. I certainly would not want to be penalized for that, and neither should this student. This dilemma places a heavy burden on the shoulders of the teacher, and frankly, it is not a situation that I had considered before participating in the practicum.

I don't know if this is applicable or not, but I know from experience that there's a chance his reading of English is better than his oral understanding of it.

—M.G.

I agree.

—G.S.

Endnote remarks by other teacher candidates:

Is Fran [Mrs. Bullock] planning on setting up separate grading criteria for him?—S.N.

Has Fran set up any meetings with the "English as a 2nd lang. teacher" at Oconee? It seems like a regular literature class is *not* the "least restrictive environment" for this boy! It's ineffective for him, & complicates class for the teacher & other students.—J.M.

What has Fran done? I like J. M.'s comment here. The student has to have his needs met, but first he must be able to comprehend the assignments. Get him to the 2nd lang. teacher. Are there any Spanish-speaking students in there? What about peer teaching techniques?—G.S.

This is a very "at-risk" student in the sense that his frustrations and problems with the language learning could ultimately turn him off of the learning process. I agree with the other comments. He needs attention before it is too late. Surely, this situation has arisen before. How was it handled then and what measures can be taken to minimize it in the future?

—M.G.

I agree with the others who've made comments. Contact ESOL teachers or somebody here at UGA for tips. You'd be surprised how his fellow students will want to help.—J.P.

---

ask for clarification about what someone had written on our papers. If we noticed that a particular topic had been addressed by several people, we could bring this up for discussion by the entire group, which often led to a deeper debate of the issue. This discussion time often led to sharing examples from our classrooms, which were usually too long to write on the Think Pieces themselves.

The Think Pieces also gave us a window into different schools, students,

Heather Ivester and Susanna Blackstone use Think Pieces to connect school experiences with campus readings.

mentor teachers, and problems encountered in other settings. We were split among several schools in urban, rural, and suburban areas. These schools offered different environments with varying problems and issues. Each school had differing racial populations and had members of varying socioeconomic backgrounds. By reading each other's Think Pieces, we encountered many different students, classrooms, and teachers. Doing so forced us to think on many different levels and to realize that there is always another way a problem can emerge and always a new way it can be overcome. Thus, although we were immersed in one school, through the Think Pieces we learned about others.

Finally, the Think Pieces offered a lasting chronicle of our personal progress as teachers and students. We are able to go back over what we have written and examine our growth, both personally and professionally. We can see how our opinions have been shaped and changed by our experiences in the classroom over time.

CRITERIA

Before we wrote our first Think Piece, our instructors gave us samples of Think Pieces written by former students. We then brainstormed a list of criteria for what we felt made "a good one." These criteria were for ourselves as readers; Think Pieces are *not* graded. We agreed that one Think Piece need not encompass all criteria but that there should be a few of the 15 criteria in each.

1. *Be honest in writing and response.* We felt that the goal of the Think Piece, that of fostering community and trust and attempting to solve problems, could be achieved only through complete sincerity on the part of both the author and the reader/respondent. Although this honesty was difficult at first because we did not want to be impolite, after the third Think Piece we knew each other well enough to overcome this inhibition.

2. *Employ humor.* The trials and tribulations we underwent seemed easier to overcome when dealt with humorously. In venting frustrations or asking for feedback on problems, we tried to remember that few things are as serious as they first seem.

3. *Share in-class examples.* When delving into problems we tried to avoid the abstract and instead give concrete examples from our classes. We believed the only way we could truly help one another was if we had as much information as possible.

4. *Be introspective/reflective.* We wanted to go beyond mere complaining toward addressing the "why" behind what was happening. We were encouraged to reflect on our situations and try to extend ourselves and grow and change; introspection and reflection were necessary to achieve this goal.

5. *Put ourselves in others' shoes.* In writing and responding to Think Pieces, we needed to empathize. When one of us was having a problem with a student or a mentor teacher, we were encouraged to put ourselves in his or her position. In reading others' Think Pieces, we tried to imagine ourselves in their situations. We felt this empathy was essential to helping each other.

6. *Vent frustration.* Many times the problems we encountered had no easy or obvious answer, or perhaps we were just upset by an encounter with a student or parent. Under these conditions, all we needed was a place to express our emotions. Many times we were comforted in having our feelings echoed by others in similar situations or in simply having a safe place in which to vent.

7. *Use open-ended questions.* As writers and as readers of Think Pieces, we tried to avoid yes–no questions as best we could and to ask questions that encouraged deep thinking. We wanted to explore beneath the surface of the

issues facing us, and as such we wanted to ask questions that encouraged discussion. Papers often began or ended with these probing questions meant to bring in our readers' opinions when we were stumped or wanted to see our own thoughts on an as yet unexamined question.

8. *Use as sounding board.* Think Pieces served as an arena in which to get feedback on new ideas. We could read each other's plans for class or possible solutions for a discipline problem and indicate whether we thought it was a good idea, warn of potential problems, or offer alternative suggestions.

9. *List solutions for commentary.* We were not to stop at compliments but to try to propose a variety of solutions. After reading of our classmates' problems, we tried to come up with practical solutions, some of which often found their way into our own classroom to be tested. For example, when a classroom management problem we had discussed surfaced in our classes, we had an arsenal of proposed solutions to try.

10. *Expand sight to other points of view.* Along with attempting to empathize with each other, our students, or our teachers, we also tried to keep an open mind and consider different ways of thinking and doing things. We wanted a variety of points of view to consider. We often referred to theories or strategies mentioned in texts and other readings we had done in an effort to connect these ideas to our lives in the classroom.

11. *Dig deeper into conversations.* Many times our talks with each other and our mentor teachers sparked conversations and ideas that did not get fleshed out fully. Think Pieces offered a place to delve into the issues we only touched on in dialogue.

12. *Do not revise.* Think Pieces were intended as an extended free-write. As such, content took precedence over form. The most important thing was to get our ideas down on paper, not to spend hours rewording and editing. As most of us typed our Think Pieces on computers, we often implemented spell-check, but this was the extent of improvement.

13. *Compare own style to mentor teacher's.* Many of us found ourselves questioning whether we wanted to teach in the same manner as our mentor teacher did. Think Pieces gave us a place to compare and contrast different teaching styles in order to work out what we liked best, as well as allowing us feedback on what others thought worked.

14. *Debate modern issues.* Several times we found modern controversy at work in our schools, with debates raging over issues like censorship, racial tensions, controversial texts, violence in the schools, or whole language. We had an opportunity to create a forum for discussing such topics in our Think Pieces each week.

15. *Go out on a limb.* Think Pieces provide a sheltered place in which to

try out unorthodox or unconventional ideas. As friends and colleagues, we could try things out on one another without fear as we struggled through defining what we believe about education.

We used these criteria as guidelines to keep in mind as we went through the process of writing out Think Pieces each week.

PROCESS

We were informed at least a week in advance whether the topic was open or one on which the entire class would focus; these two types differed greatly. An open topic meant the opportunity for each of us to explore a topic of personal concern. For example, when one of us was helping her eleventh-grade students prepare for the Georgia Writing Test, she discovered in reading the practice essays that many of them failed to include punctuation or basic subject–verb agreement. Naturally, her mind raced with questions, confusion, and even accusations. Why hadn't they learned this by now? What should she do to help them? Whose fault is it if they fail the test? The Think Piece allowed this teacher candidate to explore her own questions and options. A topic given by our instructors, on the other hand, related to an assigned reading or a research activity we had done in our classrooms. These assigned topics were sometimes more difficult, asking us to respond to the points raised in our texts or to think through a topic we had not considered before.

Once we knew the topic, we sat down to write. Using the previously mentioned criteria, we tried to work out our thoughts and feelings on the subject. We attempted to provide real examples of occurrences in classroom or real data we had collected so that our readers could identify with the experiences and respond accordingly. Although we usually vented or questioned in the beginning of the Think Piece, by the end of the process possible explanations or solutions arose along with an invitation for the reader to offer a resolution. Through Think Pieces, teacher candidates, mentor teachers, and cooperating professors created a forum where texts, theories, and classroom experiences could be shared and brought to a deeper level of understanding. Mentor teachers and professors offered insights and wisdom gained from their years of experience to the beginning teachers with whom they worked. In return they benefited from professional dialogue with the teacher candidates and with one another, seeing into the variety represented by the different schools in our program and gaining ideas for new ways of doing things in their own classrooms.

IMPLEMENTING THE THINK PIECE IN THE CLASSROOM

The most important element necessary in utilizing Think Pieces is a sense of trust and community in the classroom. Adults and teenagers alike find it difficult to share their writing with a group of unknown people. The instructor must allow the students time to get to know and trust one another before introducing them to the Think Piece process. In our class, we had spent 8 hours of class time together and shared our autobiographical portfolios with one another before we even knew we would be doing Think Pieces. Even so, the first Think Piece was difficult to do; none of us wanted to be impolite and therefore our writing and responding were a bit inhibited. However, by the third week we had spent so much time together and were so comfortable with one another that the process was unconscious. Instructors must allow students to know one another and foster an environment in which they feel comfortable sharing themselves; otherwise, the process will not work.

Another important aspect of Think Pieces is continuity. We wrote a Think Piece every week for class, and, as a result, we could look back and see how much we learned and changed over the course of the term. The Think Pieces served as wonderful indicators of growth because they were written and discussed weekly. In implementing Think Pieces, the instructor would need to set up this kind of continuity; Think Pieces do not work well if they are not done on a regular basis. Once we were into the routine, many of us knew immediately when our Think Piece topic of the week came up. Although setting up a Think Piece environment may be challenging based on work load, time, and other factors, the benefits are worth the endeavor.

CHAPTER 12

Coping with a Sense of Failure

Ginny Speaks James

Teacher candidate readers will find this chapter to be one of the most important in the book. All teachers must confront the sense that they are failing, that things just aren't working. But that is a new and frightening position to a teacher candidate. Ginny Speaks James was the first to bring her perception of this fear to the class for all of us to learn from. As Ginny's mentor teacher, Shirley Burns, explained to her, the project she tried probably wasn't as bad as she thought, and Ginny learned a lot from the experience. Here readers will get to see Ginny and Shirley's dialogue journal at work as Shirley gently—and with great patience and trust—helps Ginny negotiate the agonies of that first unit that goes far differently than she expects.

I had been in the classroom on a part-time basis for only a few weeks when my mentor teacher, Shirley Burns—or Mrs. B.—asked me to design and assign a project to accompany *Hamlet*. The students were first-period seniors, who seemed to look upon me with a mixture of amusement and disdain when I stood before them for the first time and explained that they would begin working on my project (I say "my" for obvious reasons that I will explain more fully later).

I wanted to try some of the progressive teaching methods that I had read about in *English Journal*. I figured that the way to become a great teacher was to have an arsenal of wonderful and engaging activities. My confusion was augmented with much of the theory that my classmates and I had been dipping into at the university; I was determined that I had to be Nancie Atwell (1987) or nothing. From the limited amount of literature I had read on the subject of education, I gathered that a great teacher was one who had very little direct involvement in the classroom. Most of the books that we read depicted teachers standing aside while their students conquered the great works of literature single-handedly (or in groups of their peers). I wanted to emulate these educators and treat my high school seniors as though they were college seniors. I was afraid that too much direct involvement would inhibit their creativity and sense of ownership. I guess I knew "enough to be dangerous," as the saying goes. Throughout the ordeal (as I affectionately refer to it), I recorded my progress, my students' progress, and my frustrations in a personal journal and a dialogue with Mrs. B. Excerpts from these journals illustrate my feelings and doubts in each stage of the project.

FORESHADOWING OF TROUBLE

As I previously mentioned, I already had an idea of what I wanted the *Hamlet* project to look like. I had been reading various types of educational literature on the subject of fun ways to teach Shakespeare. I came across the idea of having students rewrite the usually inaccessible lines into modern-day English. Students would break into groups (one group per act), adopt a particular style (i.e., rap, country, elite), and rewrite the lines as though they were writing a script for a modern adaptation of the play. They then would provide costumes and props appropriate to their chosen style and perform the play. I presented this idea to my students in a rapid and ill-organized manner, confusing them rather than engaging them. I had no written handout detailing the process; until much later in the project, I took it for granted that the students would be able to intuitively know what I wanted without a written handout to guide them. I suppose that I treated these adolescents as though they were adults, and assumed that they needed no written guidance. After the first brief and confusing period, Mrs. B. wrote in our dialogue journal:

> You had good information [when presenting background on Shakespeare and assigning the project]. Perhaps slowing down in your note giving would improve your presentation. When you put students into groups, you need more specific directions, written directions are needed . . . if you wait for volunteers to take acts, we'll be waiting forever! My only suggestion for improvement would be to be more specific in your directions.

These comments helped me tremendously to figure out why I was feeling so vulnerable and confused. I could not pinpoint my insecurity until it was spelled out for me; I needed those specific written directions as much as my students did. In addition to the assignment, I also gave my students a survey to complete. I was interested in monitoring their attitude toward Shakespeare and groupwork and how these attitudes would change through the course of the project. My reaction to these surveys is documented in my personal journal:

Their surveys indicated that most of them felt positively about it. The only thing I did wrong was I was not well-prepared. I got them into groups, but I didn't have any specific written instruction for them—I didn't even think about it! I realize they may need (and want) more structure. I can understand how they feel!

I did understand how they felt. I was feeling as lost and confused as they were. I sensed that I was floundering in the classroom. My insecurities about my own abilities as a teacher began to surface. I was having a difficult time reconciling the wonderful stories of Atwellian teachers turning their classrooms into forums for discovery, independence, and excitement with the reality that students do not automatically cooperate (if they do at all), and that the undertaking of becoming an educator consisted of much more than pulling a rabbit out of a hat; I soon discovered that, as a magician labors to create the illusion that his craft materializes from midair, so must a teacher toil to create an "effortless" classroom. This project was my first glimpse into the complex world of teaching.

TROUBLE REALIZED

The *Hamlet* project was under way, and I began to have strong misgivings about the progress made so far. The students were to work on the project on Mondays and Wednesdays (the only days that I was in the school) during class. I soon realized that the time available to students to work on the project was not nearly enough. Also, because I saw them only twice a week, I found it extremely difficult to communicate with them about due dates and expectations. I started writing them memos, which gave them the written instructions they needed; however, it became apparent that it was too late. The project spanned only a 4-week period, which gave the students approximately seven class periods to work (the first day was spent on background information and the assignment). I had unrealistic expectations of what this group of teenagers would be able to accomplish in such a brief period; I secretly hoped that they would work on it independently. Most of my misconceptions were based simply on my lack of experience and education. I came into the classroom cold, and I did not yet have the instincts that most teachers develop regarding what their students can or will do.

Specifically, each group was to rewrite its entire act into modern dialect. Then, each student in the group was to assume a character and perform the act in costume. I allowed one of the students in each group to be the director if he or she did not feel comfortable performing or if there were not enough characters for each person to have a part. The rewrites were originally due one week after assignment, but after the students begged, I ended up giving extensions. It did no good. I had only two students (out of 22) turn in their rewritten acts. I had never modeled or explained how to rewrite the lines, and I also had assumed that the students would get the gist of the lines and pick and choose which ones to rewrite. I told them that they did not have to rewrite every single line; they had a great deal of freedom in their interpretations. I encouraged them to shorten an entire act into a single page or two, but the two rewrites that I did receive were rewritten line by line. One group practically copied the entire act word for word. This was not what I wanted, but I could not make the students understand that this project should be fun, not tedious and painstaking.

The students began complaining constantly. Because they were working in groups, each student depended on the rest of the students in the group to complete their parts. The few diligent students who turned in their rewrites complained that the rest of the students in the group were not doing their parts. I grew tired of hearing the complaining and whining, so I became impatient and intolerant. Because I was unsure about the project that I had assigned haphazardly, I felt guilty and allowed the students to turn in things late. At this point in my preteaching career, I had not considered that it is perfectly acceptable to abort a mission that is clearly headed for disaster. My mounting frustration is evident in my journal entries during the third harrowing week:

> It's so frustrating because I don't know how to make them turn in their projects. They don't seem terribly motivated by grades, and threats work only minimally. Some of them are conscientious and creative, but a few are acting like brats! It may sound bad, but I kind of wish it was over already.

Upon reading these entries, it becomes evident that I was operating under a crucial flaw: I was not consulting my students. It seems so obvious now, but it was something that I easily overlooked as I attempted to mold and shape them into excited and conscientious students who would adhere to the project with a zealous appreciation of Shakespeare and me. If I had once asked myself, "Why are these students resisting this idea so much?" I could have dropped the project long before I did. I was on the brink of learning an invaluable lesson in teaching, a lesson that would become a guiding force in my teaching for the rest of the year. However, I still had *Hamlet* with which to contend.

Three weeks into the project, I was still making concessions to my students. I had extended the performance deadline 3 weeks, more for myself than for them, because I wanted so badly for this project to succeed the way that I had planned it. Although my students gave no indication that they were making a concerted effort to procure costumes and props, somehow this did not faze me. I was wrapped securely in the notion that it would all work out (or that it would at least be over). On the fateful day, however, only one group seemed ready to perform their act. Some groups just turned in their rewritten lines, and many were absent from school altogether. At that point I lost it. My journal from that day reads:

> I'm so frustrated I could cry. The students will not do anything I ask them today. They've had about 3 extra weeks to do these rewrites (I've given them 2 weeks extra!) but I'm still missing some! . . . I'm so mad! . . . I'm trying to work with them, but they won't all cooperate.

My dialogue journal with Mrs. B. shows my pleading and guilt during this time:

> First period is driving me crazy! I don't know what to do. . . . I know I'm giving them too many chances. I don't know why. . . . I think I may feel kinda bad—I mean, I loaded them with this project, I really don't know what I'm doing, and they're probably as confused as I am. This project is worrying me *to death.* I guess maybe I feel like, if I fail them, I fail, too.

FINDING MY WAY OUT

The notion that failure is not the end of the world was a new idea for me. I read *Making the Journey* by Leila Christenbury (1994) and several articles in *English Journal,* and I heard over and over that it is all right, maybe even preferable, to bail out of a lesson that is not going well. I learned that I should not punish myself for a failure that I had made out of sheer inexperience; instead, I should act immediately to rectify what I had done and salvage a lesson out of the experience for myself and my students. That is precisely what I did.

After the group that had completed their project performed their act, I made a split-second decision that was probably the best I had made since entering the classroom 2 months earlier. I decided that the class could still turn in their rewritten acts for half of the project grade and could complete some sort of individual project related to *Hamlet* for their performance half of the grade. I hated to let this happen, because I felt as if I were giving in to their laziness and apathy. I also had to swallow my pride; I loathed the idea that they would think that they had forced me to give in and that I had failed. I later found out that I had nothing to fear; they neither judged me nor ridiculed me for my failure. They were honest and forthright in their evaluation of what I had done.

Regardless of how they felt about me as a teacher, I felt a tremendous sense of relief as a result of "jumping ship" on the *Hamlet* ordeal. After Mrs. B. consoled me, I responded in my dialogue journal:

> Thanks for making me feel a little better about the project. I'm glad to know that I'm not the only one who wasn't 100% successful in group-work. I think, had I approached them a little differently and been a little better organized, I could have gotten them at least somewhat interested.

That entry is quite an understatement as I reflect upon that experience now. I finally realized that clinging to a lesson or project that the students hate is fighting a losing battle. It was taking its toll on me, my students, and our relationship. My underlying interest in assigning a group project was to enable me to get to know them better and to develop a closer relationship among them. What I managed to do, however, was to isolate myself from them and create a tension in the classroom that began to dissipate only when I gave up the project.

The difference that day was amazing. Students who previously had given me looks of resentment were friendly and open. Even though a large portion of the class did not complete the individual project, they knew that the responsibility finally lay with them, and they did not seem to resent me the way they had the previous few months. I can say honestly that giving up the lesson was the best thing I did during my student teaching.

STUDENT INSIGHT

Perhaps the most humbling, and educating, experience of all came when I asked the students to write a journal entry giving me an honest and constructive opinion of what I did wrong and what I could do in the future to make this kind of project successful and interesting. The responses astounded me, and I truly understood how much the students themselves know about education. While I was spending all those weeks lying in bed at night wondering what I was doing wrong, the students knew the answers all along. The following excerpts are the small, but not insignificant, bits of wisdom that my students gave to me.

Chris: Personally, I think that the idea for the play was great!! The reason I think that they did not work out is because we didn't have enough time in class to work on them. It was impossible for us to work as a group at home due to lack of communication. But I wish that it would've worked out because it would've been lots of fun.

John: I liked the *Hamlet* project ideas but I didn't like that it wasn't really organized. It was an easy grade, and God knows we need some easy As. I wish that we could have had some other way of acting the rewrites. In all it was a good idea.

Allison: I liked this project, because we got to work in groups. I think it would have been put together better if we would have worked in class a little more. The only thing I didn't like was the fact that some people didn't show up today, but that is not your fault, that's ours.

Dana: I think that this project could have been done in a different way. Instead of everyone writing lines, it may have been a little easier if we wrote our own parts. Then we could have read our parts even if the other person was out. We would also have known more about what was going on.

Jeff: I think this project would have turned out better if you got more cooperation out of the class. I think it was fun. It would have been more fun if we could have acted it out in front of the camera. Part of the reason people did not want to do it is because they are camera shy. I know you will become a good teacher. You just have to be mean at first to show the students you mean business and then you can be nice. Then they will know if they cross you they will regret it.

Although some of the students may have been a little excessive in their advice, overall they gave me concrete suggestions on how to assign a performance-based project with a Shakespearean play. Several months later, I read educational literature on teaching Shakespeare that contained the same advice that my students provided. Since then, I have learned a variety of techniques based on rewriting and performing Shakespearean plays. These are modifications of my own idea, which seem much more doable for students. If I had used one of these techniques, I believe that I could have executed a successful project without the headaches and guilt that I experienced. I do not regret that the project failed, because my students taught me more about myself and education than any teaching manual could have.

REFLECTION: TWO YEARS LATER

Here I am, over 2 years later, a second-year English teacher. As I reflect on my humbling experiences as a teacher candidate, I must admit that my memories of the *Hamlet* project are somewhat bittersweet. Despite those uncomfortable memories, I feel that the experience taught me lessons beyond the realm of failure alone. I actually learned a great deal about myself through the experience. I realized that I am, by nature, unorganized, spontaneous, and laid back. Although I suppose I always knew these things, they suddenly revealed themselves in my teaching style, causing my students and me (and poor Shirley) some trouble. I also have come to understand that who I am as a person will never change. What's more, I'm not sure that I really *want* to change. I have learned to harness the quirks that make me a unique human being, as well as a good teacher.

Since I began my teaching job almost 2 years ago, I have developed a system that works for me. Almost immediately it became apparent that I had to learn new organizational skills. Because of the tremendous amount of paperwork from administrators and students, I needed to develop a system that would enable me to get everything done. When it comes to this facet of the job, my sanity depends on writing down everything (appointments, due dates, daily lesson plans, and so forth). This is where my fly-by-the-seat-of-my-pants attitude had to change, for my own sanity as well as that of my colleagues and students. However, when it comes to the actual *teaching* aspect of my career, I still rely on my spontaneous nature to get me through. I must formulate a loose plan for the entire quarter; this includes what novel(s) we'll read and when we'll read them. Planning these types of things far in advance is a necessity when there are a limited number of books and several other teachers want to teach them the same quarter. Beyond that, I plan in some detail about a week in advance. However, the same mindset that got me in hot water during the *Hamlet* unit allows me to be flexible within those plans. Assemblies, fire drills, and other unforeseen events can disrupt and upset teachers who are more rigid and structured by nature. I, however, handle them pretty well. I have little trouble putting off a lesson or creating an alternative lesson plan at the spur of the moment. Also, because I learned to handle failure early in my preservice career, I have no problem admitting that a lesson simply is not working and switching gears because of that flexibility.

Another lesson that my *Hamlet* experience taught me was that it is imperative to write down all instructions when assigning a project or other activity. For some reason, students seem to believe that instructions that are typed, printed, and photocopied are somehow more valid and important than those that are given verbally or written on the chalkboard for them to copy into their notes. Had I done this for the *Hamlet* project, many of my problems could have been prevented.

Most important, I came to realize that I can prevent some classroom disasters by simply asking my students if a lesson is working; if they say "no," then I can move on to something else. I thank my teacher education, and particularly my mentor teacher, for that valuable skill. Although I had to learn that the hard way, I am glad that I learned it! Students will be brutally honest about your performance as an educator if you give them a chance!

REFERENCES

Atwell, N. (1987). *In the middle: Writing, reading, and learning with adolescents.* Portsmouth, NH: Boynton/Cook.

Christenbury, L. (1994). *Making the journey: Being and becoming a teacher of English language arts.* Portsmouth, NH: Boynton/Cook.

CHAPTER 13

Discipline: Early Fears and Later Realities

Jennifer McDuffie Stewart

Like many student teachers, Jennifer was concerned about how to establish herself as an authority figure with her teenage students. In the first part of this chapter, Jennifer talks about her fears and realities as a student teacher who wanted an effective discipline plan that would create the climate she sought for herself and her students. Now, several years of teaching experience allow her to reflect on those early fears and the ways she has found to address discipline as a second-year teacher.

I enter the classroom immediately after the bell rings ready to greet my students on the first day of school. I have my plans, a positive attitude, and enough idealistic optimism for 10 teachers. I put my gradebook down and ask everyone nicely to sit down so we can get started. Nobody looks at me. I raise my voice.

"Please sit down so I can take attendance."

I see a jumbo-size paper airplane flying right toward my head and I duck.

"Have a seat now!" I see it is time to be firm.

The noise is growing, a desk is overturned, and two boys are fighting in the back of the room. A couple of girls walk out of the room, walking past me as though I am not even there.

"What's going on here?! I'm the teacher! You're supposed to listen to me. Why isn't anybody listening to me?"

This is the dream/nightmare I had every night for the 2 weeks before I began student teaching. My fear of losing (or never gaining) control of the classroom invaded every aspect of my life during that time. I worried about not being taken seriously by the students, not being able to handle the disruptions I felt sure would occur, and not being able to "make" the students behave.

I knew I would be teaching all tenth graders, 15- and 16-year-olds who just recently had begun to think they were old enough to decide what they were going to do, but who, in reality, still needed a lot of guidance and help. I read several books on discipline and classroom management, including *The First Days of School* (Wong & Wong, 1991) and *Discipline with Dignity* (Curwin & Mendler, 1988). From these books, I developed my first plan of action: two posters to hang on the wall of my classroom that covered the rules and consequences.

Rules for Our Classroom

1. Bring all necessary materials to class daily.
2. No personal grooming in class.
3. Arrive at class on time daily.
4. Show respect to everyone.

Consequences

First time: Warning, name on board
Second time: 15 minutes after school, check by name
Third time: 30 minutes after school, check by name, call to parents
Fourth time: Sent to office

Just looking at this now makes me both laugh and sigh with relief that I never actually showed the posters to my students. I know now I would have been either laughed out of the room or hospitalized due to the inordinate amount of stress this policy would have caused.

But initially I did believe this would work. I felt it covered all of the bases adequately and fairly. There would be no way to argue with this plan when the rules and consequences were posted up on the wall. I could follow the same steps for every student and for every misdemeanor. I showed this "technique" to my mentor teacher, and, to his credit, he did not point out any problems with it. He let me find out things for myself, and if that meant bombing hard, then I would just remember that lesson all the better.

For some reason, these posters stayed in the back of my mind while my student teaching period was drawing closer and closer. Something did not seem right, but I could not put a finger on it. Then, the day before I began, I realized what it was. The technique was not mine. I had taken four random rules and four strict consequences out of a book and had not created a way to adapt it to *my* techniques as a teacher. It just was not me, and it would never work, for two main reasons.

First, having those four consequences for those four specific rules would put me in the position of playing police in the classroom. Did I really want to have to turn around and put checks on the board every 5 or 10 minutes? Did I really want to have to give a student detention for brushing his or her hair? With some students I suppose such strict policies would be needed, but I had seen my students in action and there were no major problems. Therefore, I decided that for my classes, such measures would not be necessary.

Second, the four consequences were to be set in concrete. They allowed no room for individualization, and this, I learned quickly, is a must in any classroom. I learned that each student is different and has different circumstances, and they must be treated as such. One thing I can do as a teacher is to try to be *fair*. Fair for one child will be different for another. But with such strict consequences, there was no room for such allowances.

The day before my student teaching began, I knew I had to start from scratch and develop a plan that I really believed in.

Having discussed what I didn't do, let me move on to what I did try. As I said, each day was different. Depending on my mood, my students, and the advice I happened to receive, I tried different techniques to see which ones worked for us and which ones didn't. It was definitely a trial and error process.

I began by working on my "teacher voice": the voice of authority. This was hard for me initially because I have a fairly quiet voice, and I do not like to yell. So I practiced speaking with authority: not making every statement end up sounding like a question; not mumbling when I was talking one-on-one with a student. This was easier to get used to than I thought, I suppose because it seemed like a matter of necessity. If I sounded unsure of myself or shy, the students would pick up on it immediately.

What was much harder for me to be aware of and improve was body language. One of the *best* things to do during student teaching is to videotape yourself. It's the most effective way to see yourself as the students see you. I did this numerous times, and although I was usually so embarrassed with the result that I immediately erased the episode, it was very helpful. It allowed me to see that when I sit on a desk with my legs crossed during a discussion, I look like a small, nervous student. When I twirl a pencil in my hand as I'm asking questions, I look uncomfortable. When a student approaches me and I take a step backward, I look intimidated. It was all so obvious on tape, but it was the little nervous habits that I didn't even realize I was doing that were making me look out of place in front of the students.

I took each of these step by step. When I was observed, I would ask the person to watch to see if I fiddled with pens or pencils. I would ask them to watch my body language when I spoke to a student who needed help, came in late, or was not following directions. I cannot stress enough how much these videos and observations helped. They forced me to pay attention to what I was *doing* and not just what I was *saying*.

As for "dealing" with the students, I began the quarter by explaining the discipline plan we were going to have. This part was tricky, because in my case the students had already been in the classroom for about 7 months. I felt strongly that if I were to come in with a *strict* or harsh discipline policy (sort of like those posters I originally intended to use), the students would "turn" on me. After all, I was the new leader in class. I learned quickly that students *do not* like it when a student teacher comes in and changes everything.

I told them that our rule was to *respect others.* This included all of the basics, which we went over, such as getting to class on time, not talking when others are talking, and so forth. I said I would give one warning whenever the rule was broken and then would give detention the next time it happened. I think that this was a very fair and workable plan. Unfortunately, I did not follow it as strictly as I should have. Too many times I told one student to be quiet six or seven times in one period and never followed through with the consequence. This definitely would be something I would change if I could do it over again. Stick with the plan!!! If you don't follow through with it, the students won't either.

My main method of quieting students (especially right at the beginning of the period) was to stand at the podium and wait for them to get quiet. Although there were no direct consequences for failing to get quiet, students responded to avoid being "caught" talking after everyone else had become quiet. This always worked because within 1 or 2 minutes, a few students would notice that it was time to be quiet and would tell their friends to be quiet. Unfortunately, this technique would drive my students crazy. "Y'all be quiet," they'd say, "so she'll quit standing up there watching us!"

Then one day, I was standing in front of the room waiting for them to stop talking. Suddenly, Lauren, who always seemed to be the last one to realize that I was standing in front waiting for their attention, decided that it was time to negotiate my procedure. Because she never realized that I was standing in front, she thought it would work better if I also would give the class a verbal warning, in case they didn't see me. I thought this sounded fair. Actually, it made a lot of sense. So we sort of reached a compromise. I would say, "This is your warning!" and then stand quietly until they stopped talking.

I'm not sure that this would work in all situations. My students were motivated to stop talking because they would all ask, "What are we doing today?" or "Why are the desks set up like this?" and the only answer I would give was, "I'll tell you as soon as everyone is quiet." They hated not knowing what was going on so that approach always worked.

I think that this is one of the most valuable, practical lessons I learned about getting students to behave. If I could keep them interested and busy, I had fewer problems. If the lessons were engaging, even the most disruptive students would express interest, especially if groupwork or some type of competitive work was involved. None of them wanted to have a team member "mess them up," so they did a very effective job of keeping each other in line.

One other technique that I found to be very successful was to speak to the student causing trouble one-on-one, rather than confronting him or her in front of the class. When I would confront Greg for talking, he immediately would say one of two things: "I was *not* talking! I didn't say anything!" or "Everybody else is talking, too. Why are you only yelling at me?" However, when I would walk over to Greg and whisper the same thing to him or talk to him right after class was over, he would acknowledge that he had been disruptive and would even promise to try to be better the rest of class or the next day. The difference was amazing. Without all of their friends listening and judging, students were much more agreeable and willing to work out the problem.

During detention, after having time to think about the situation, is the perfect time to talk to a student about a problem, like the one I had with a student named Anthony. He was a big boy, a football player, and had a deep, booming voice. He constantly got in trouble, and I finally gave him a very well-deserved detention. He came in before school for 45 minutes. We spent 5 minutes discussing what he had done and why, and another 5 minutes discussing why he thought I was being unfair (he felt I called on him for talking too much; I had to explain that he was always talking and that his voice was much louder than everyone else's in the class). We worked out an agreement: He would try to stop talking when another student or I was talking, and I would try to stop calling his name out in class. Instead I would give him a look or walk by and tap him on the shoulder. We decided this was fair, and then spent the last 30 minutes of his detention talking about his job and what was going on with his family and the work he needed to do on his truck and so on. After that day, Anthony and I did not have any more problems.

Discipline was an ongoing issue for me. I learned something new every day; it was definitely a trial and error process. However, I think I learned the most the last week of school when I asked my students to fill out my evaluations. The advice they gave on what works and what doesn't for a teacher was invaluable. Some of the evaluations were contradictory, and some of them I had a hard time agreeing with, but they were all interesting considering that they came straight from the source!

I suggest surveying each class you have to find out what works best for you and your students. The following five suggestions from students are the ones I found to be the most helpful for me:

1. You need to be more firm. Raise your voice! Don't tolerate those, like me, who enjoy misbehaving. (Throw them out of class and let administration handle it.)

2. If you respect students they will respect you back.

3. Waiting for the class to be quiet worked because we eventually got quiet.

4. Call out names of students talking. (This was a common answer from many students.)

5. I have found that the foremost effective discipline on me is when the teacher quietly takes me outside and discusses specifically what I have done wrong and how I should change. When teachers do this I really respect them more than if they had embarrassed me. Respect is important in teaching, and I usually don't harbor hard feelings for a teacher who does this.

REFLECTION: TWO YEARS LATER

Discipline is no longer the pressing (perhaps smothering would be more accurate) issue it was during my student teaching experience. Of course, it's still a major concern I deal with on a daily basis, but it is definitely on more of a one-on-one level, as opposed to discipline for the class as a whole. I assume there will always be individual cases that may catch me off guard, and I may always question the way I handle each one, wondering if there isn't a better way to solve the problem. As for managing the class as a whole, however, I have found several procedures with which my students and I are comfortable.

I begin each year with a seating chart. I change this around throughout the course of the year (to fend off discipline problems and boredom), but I always have assigned seating. In addition, during the first week of school, I can associate faces and names with certain seats or rows. I usually learn the majority of names on the first day of school. I feel strongly that this both shows the students that I am interested in them and cuts down on minor discipline problems, because I can call the "offending" student by name.

Other procedures that work for me are asking students to be at their desks when the bell rings. Fortunately, this is a school rule, so all I have to do is enforce it. Not being at the desk results in a tardy; after four tardies, a student is disciplined by an administrator. Starting out the class period in an orderly fashion is very important. It definitely sets the tone for the remainder of the class. There is also a procedure for the end of class. I explain to students that I dismiss the class; the bell does not. No more lining up at the door, waiting for the bell to ring; all students must be at their desks.

Most discipline problems that occur are fairly minor. Depending on the students, I either call them by name or talk to them quietly at their desks. It usually does not take long to figure out to which type of corrective procedure each student responds best. If the problem is severe, I try to remove the student from the situation by sending him or her out into the hall. After allowing a minute or two to "cool down," I step out to talk to the student, being careful to pursue the situation in an understanding, as opposed to accusing, manner. In anticipation of the possible persistence of problems, I keep a notebook documenting all discipline situations that occur during class. If the need arises, I will turn a student over to an administrator, along with a comprehensive list of offenses the student has been involved in.

I realized quickly that for me the best way to control discipline is to show the students that I care and that I am fair. I establish a relationship with each student during the semester, so that if someone does get in trouble, that student will trust that I will handle the situation in the best manner possible.

REFERENCES

Curwin, R. L., & Mendler, A. N. (1988). *Discipline with dignity* (2nd ed.). Alexandria, VA: Association for Supervision and Curriculum Development.

Wong, H. K., & Wong, P. (1991). *The first days of school.* Sunnyvale, CA: Harry Wong.

CHAPTER 14

How to Lead a Classroom Discussion

Elaine Perry & Greg Slattery

Teacher candidates Elaine and Greg learned how to lead discussions of shared classroom texts from experiences with their ninth- and twelfth-grade students, respectively. In this chapter, they share the nitty-gritty details that beginners crave, a guide for setting up, leading, and reflecting on whole class discussions. In her reflection, Elaine, now an eighth-grade teacher, talks about how she's made transitions for the needs of middle-grade learners and as a result of her own professional growth. Experienced readers, who now lead discussions intuitively, will see again this difficult concept from the perspective of beginners. They also may pick up a few good ideas themselves.

BACKGROUND/BURNING QUESTIONS

Elaine

While planning a unit on *To Kill a Mockingbird* for ninth graders, I allotted, without hesitation, several days for classroom discussions because there were so many characterization, thematic, and social issues worthy of discussion. Of course, I wanted students to move beyond recall and comprehension levels, and I thought it was important for them to be able to communicate their views verbally, as well as in writing.

Each advanced class had approximately 30 students with little or no experience in large group discussions. These were very bright students who had such valuable things to say; however, they all wanted to say them at once and be heard. I felt that many of the students listened solely to me to get their valuable information. Technically, they listened to two people, themselves and me. It was like they each wanted to have a conversation with me—each conversation in and of itself, not recognized, developed, or affected by any other.

I became consumed with several questions. Why do I find myself constantly repeating good comments made by the students? (The student made the statement, and if everyone had been listening intently, then the comment would have been heard. I realized that my repeating the comment didn't automatically make it significant.) How do you make them listen to each other? Why does the conversation end up so disjointed? How can we structure or organize the discussion so that *everyone* benefits?

Greg

Before beginning student teaching, I knew I wanted to create classrooms where there was a great deal of discussion. I did not want to be a "lecture" teacher all the time. Open discussion can and should be a vital part of any study of literature. I was determined to have a classroom that included that strategy.

With that philosophy in hand, I entered the real world of student teaching. Our first day together my senior-year students were not prepared to discuss anything. It was so odd; before class started, the room was filled with discussion. When I asked the first question, I got silence. I plowed through the rest of the class time expecting it to get better as the day went along. It didn't. By the end of the first hour, it was obvious that the students and I needed to talk about discussion. Their biggest question nearly blew me away: "Why do we even need to have discussion?" This question really made me stop and think about why I wanted to teach using discussion as a major teaching strategy, how to make the students believe it was important, and how to make sure the students understood how I expected a discussion to be carried out.

After the miserable failure of the first attempt at classroom discussion, I had to explain to my students why I believed in classroom discussion—the easiest part of my explanation to them. Literature should do more than merely present the characters, settings, and plot. The ultimate goal of literature is to make the student think. It should make the student think about how this particular piece of literature can relate to his or her personal life. It is only when the literature is made relevant to students that they will realize ownership of that literature. One of the best techniques I have seen for creating this ownership is classroom discussion.

Another, more pressing concern for the students was to apply classroom discussion to test grades. Students did not understand why they needed to be able to discuss themes or lines in literature to do well on an objective test. I had to explain to them that my tests were not going to be objective. There wouldn't be any multiple choice or true–false questions. The students immediately made the connection between doing a better job in class discussions and doing better on tests. This line of thinking gave rise to the inevitable questions, "Who's right?" and "Who decides who's right?"

The students and I arrived at logical answers to both questions. Any answer potentially could be correct as long as it could be supported with quotes or lines from the particular text we were reading. An answer was deemed incorrect only if there wasn't any evidence to support it.

SETUP FOR DISCUSSIONS

Elaine

Very few worthwhile discussions stem from nowhere. There needs to be some sort of basis for discussion. It helps if the students have "tools" in front of them to guide them in a sense.

In their response journals, students kept a list of ideas and insights they might write about later. I had given them an extensive list of essay topics early on in the unit to help them know what to focus on while reading. I also had given them "prompts" to respond to at pivotal points. Thus, each student had very personal and individualized notes and reactions to what he or she was reading. Since they had already addressed many of the issues in writing, the journal served as a helpful tool in verbalizing their views. It was not a crutch, but a guide when they needed one, a handy way to find concrete examples or recall initial reactions.

Greg

Originally (naively), I expected to come in, ask a question, sit back, and enjoy the discussion. As you can imagine, it didn't happen that way. After failing more than once to make the students understand what I wanted them to be able to discuss during class time, I began sending home a set of questions that they had to answer before class the next day. The students were still hesitant to really speak up about what they believed. Our teacher education classroom discussions at the university went from small group to large group, so I tried that technique next.

We finally arrived! The final step to creating the classroom discussion was at hand. To set up the discussion, the students had to have a set of questions that they could attempt to answer on their own at home prior to coming to class, *and* they had to have the opportunity to share their answers in a smaller setting before presenting their ideas to the class.

On campus, small group discussions prepare teacher candidates to participate in large group dialogue. *Left to right,* Niki Arnold, Leta Tipton (teacher-visitor), Sean Michael, and Heather Bickerstaff.

HOW-TO'S FOR DISCUSSIONS

Elaine

Shortly after we'd begun the *To Kill a Mockingbird* unit, our first large group discussion day arrived. I knew that the first thing was to agree on what makes a good group discussion or, in other words, the actual "mechanics" to make it run smoothly.

First and foremost, I had to emphasize the importance of *listening,* a concept that's easy to take for granted. I thoroughly explained several components of a good discussion: *bouncing, elaborating, connecting,* and *clarifying.*

We talked about the "bouncing" effect that should occur. If one student said something that triggered a disagreement, an agreement, or an elaboration, then that was the perfect opportunity for another to respond or react to that. If only they would listen to each other and recognize those cues (opportunities), the conversation would flow so much more smoothly, and they would learn so much more by "bouncing" off each other.

My ninth graders were so used to simply making a statement and stopping. I wanted them to understand that if you have something valuable to say and you want to be taken seriously, you have to back up what you say with specifics. At first, when I used the word "elaborate" after a short response to urge them to talk more, they uttered one or two extra phrases, thinking I was testing or judging them. By the time we had had several discussions, they learned that they didn't need to elaborate just to appease me but to make their expressions stronger.

"Connecting" was another concept we talked about beforehand. I believe that sometimes students hold their views and ideas so within themselves that they claim ownership and are reluctant to have their ideas elaborated on, challenged, or modified in any way. I explained to them that in large group discussions, connections are what it's all about. It's okay, in fact, it's wonderful for them and their peers to make connections and build on them. Greater understanding and, at the very least, reassurance can result.

Often, a teacher is called upon by the students to explain or "clarify" what he or she means. So, it is not unreasonable that in a classroom discussion, students should be prepared, or almost eager, to clarify what they say. We discussed the importance of using concrete examples from the text or any other source to substantiate their claims. Above all, the students should realize that it's their responsibility to clarify their statements and reactions.

I wanted our discussions to be smooth and free flowing, not confining and methodical. For ninth graders, though, turn taking is not natural; it has to be practiced. They don't always have the patience to speak one at a time or to seize nonverbal cues, so I encouraged them to raise their hands to be called on. I also made it clear that one person had the floor at a time.

To avoid a number of students sitting there indefinitely with their hands raised, I called several names in the order in which they could speak. This helped to cut down on the frustration some eager students might have had to "get it out." After recognizing them by name, they knew they would have their say, so they didn't have the attitude of "well, just forget it." My goal was to get them so used to bouncing, elaborating, connecting, and clarifying that they gradually would be able to move toward nonverbal cues and more subtle shifts.

Greg

I wish I could say that every discussion we had after those first successes went well. I wish I could say that the first day I tried it everything went great. But . . . after deciding how to set up the class for discussion, we still had to make the discussion flow.

Initially, I elected to stay away from hand raising. My students were seniors, and I thought we would be able to dispense with that. I quickly realized that they were incapable of this. Without hand raising, discussion quickly turned to several small discussions. These were usually relevant discussions, yet they did little to benefit the entire class.

We went to hand raising. I tried to call one student at a time; I allowed the students to call on the next person. I found this approach unwieldy and it did, in fact, limit discussion. Students refused to wait their turn, they talked over each other, and at times they lost interest while awaiting their turn to add something meaningful. I tried calling several names at once, and that alleviated the problem, but did not eliminate it altogether. I finally hit on two methods that made the best of organization and spontaneity.

As I called on students to respond, I asked them to respond to the previous statement or question. This made the student at least hesitate before blurting out opinions. The two most frequent expressions in my vocabulary became, "Why . . . Casey?" and "Build on that . . . Jason." I coupled this with my own continual movement that allowed proximity to negate a great deal of excess conversation. The students quickly understood that any statement would have to be supported, and they spent more time attempting to think things out.

TEACHER'S ROLE AS LEADER OF DISCUSSION

Elaine

The more discussions we had and the more we concentrated on the students' roles, the more I learned about the role I needed to play. I learned that the teacher is not there to control the conversation but to facilitate it. As a leader of discussion, you have an obligation to respond to what you hear, not just what you want to hear. You need to be able to make connections when students may not be and to recognize significant points in their conversations to "bridge" and open up other possibilities. It's important to push students to explore what they say and mean instead of jumping in with your interpretation of what they say, and to add clarification rather than dictate meaning. Overall, I believe that the most important thing is to learn to listen to your students and let their input guide you, instead of just blocking them out and trying to stick to an agenda that should guide them.

Greg

Discussion in a classroom is essential and can be incredibly powerful in making a work relevant to a student's life. Initially my "discussions" sounded more like lectures because I attempted to control the discussions to make the students see what I thought was important, instead of allowing them to discover what they thought was important. My role turned into that of facilitator instead of lecturer. The most difficult point in "leading" the discussion came in releasing control. I learned that the students occasionally needed me to help make connections or to push them into the deeper meanings. More important, I learned that if I was patient enough, they would take the literature and make it theirs.

SUMMARY

Elaine

All of the classroom discussions went well, and I was continually impressed with the students' perceptions and ability to relate their experiences to the novel. The most rewarding experience was on our final discussion day of *To Kill a Mockingbird,* near the end of the quarter as we embarked on a discussion about the outcome of the Tom Robinson trial, the attitudes of Maycomb's citizens, and the mockingbird motif. What ensued that day was so much more than I had ever wished for. My fifth-period class dived into these issues and more. They voiced their opinions about the trial and speculated on the different characters' reactions and what behaviors revealed those reactions. Some students disagreed with one student's remarks about Atticus, and another questioned why he thought that. Before my very eyes, several students opened their novel and spouted off quotes to support their opinions. They argued different interpretations of certain passages. Another student flipped back in his response journal to share one reaction he had before he read the verdict and then flipped ahead to a later reaction to compare them. The students were challenging one another and pushing each other to prove their points. I heard students providing the cues that I was accustomed to giving. The energy in the room was so great and so positive. It wasn't until after the bell had rung that I realized something else. Students had started the discussion by raising hands as they usually did, but somewhere along the way they didn't have to. They had mastered recognizing those nonverbal cues and took opportunities when they could. Thirty of us had had a phenomenal conversation that *not once* bordered on chaos.

I strongly believe that large group discussions in the English classroom are very beneficial because they give 30 readers of a common text the opportunity to create relevance and make connections. Each student brings his or her own knowledge, experiences, and interpretations to an open forum of conversation, and their exposure to those similarities and differences can only broaden their understanding and sharpen their critical thinking skills.

Greg

Gradually, the need for my prompts and proximity diminished. Discussion flowed, although at times it was more like a river flowing through a gorge than the quiet orderly mountain stream I envisioned. Yet the more I thought about the great discussions I had participated in, the more I realized that they were often full of sound and fury. Students respond when they realize that their voice will be heard and their opinions will count, and they have clear guidelines and expectations. Our routine for discussion became orderly as the students worked in small groups to hammer out the questions in their own minds before they were brought before the entire group. Allowing them to discuss in their own small groups, and then prodding, pushing, and pulling them into discussion in a large group, was a tremendous tool for learning.

REFLECTION: TWO YEARS LATER

Elaine: Adapting Strategies to Eighth Graders

As I embarked on my first year teaching eighth graders, classroom discussions still remained high on my priority list of activities I wanted the students to engage in on a regular basis. Although there was only a year's difference between this age group and the group that I had student taught, I quickly realized that I would face many more issues with the eighth graders than I had with my first-year high school students.

The same concerns still guided me as I planned discussions with them:

- How can we make these discussions worthwhile?
- Will a few flamboyant students monopolize the conversation?
- What about the unusually quiet, yet extremely bright kids?
- What will keep all of them actively listening?

After working with the 13-year-olds in a classroom setting, I had already observed that I would have to modify my strategies a bit. Eighth grade is an awkward time when adolescents are going through so many hormonal and emotional changes and at such different paces. I found that large group discussions were even more difficult to facilitate because the students did not have the same goals for the activity that I had. They seemed unusually egocentric and very socially conscious. Some were concerned about sounding really intelligent (even if that meant just spouting off one really good line a period). Such a student would then bask in his "fame" and not feel the need to utter another word for the rest of the period. Others didn't want to say anything too smart for fear of being labeled "nerdy." Most common, though, were the students who loved to hear themselves talk or the ones who loved to chime in at an "opportune" time to crack a joke and get a laugh. I knew that before we tried the discussion in a large group setting they needed to work on the concepts in small groups. I hoped this would help eliminate the "stage" facade before they had a chance to get really misdirected.

Therefore, after our lesson on the "do's and don'ts" (incidentally, I felt they needed to take notes on the whole process), I organized them into groups of three to four students based on several factors—ability, personality, social relationships, and so forth. This was a tedious process because I wanted the small groups to be an optimal environment for them to benefit from a discussion of a text, and there were so many factors that could interfere with that. For example, they couldn't leave their grudges for particular students at the door or put their boyfriend/girlfriend relationships aside, so I couldn't very well ignore such relationships either (at least not at this early stage).

Over the next few months as opportunities arose, we tried the small group discussions. They had to be reminded of *my* (not yet "*our*") goals—bouncing, elaborating, connecting, and clarifying. They needed lots of practice in the smaller setting before we tried it as a whole class.

Ultimately, we did embark on several large group discussions, and after much patience and reminding, they were successful. Had they not been able to "train themselves" in smaller groups, I know these eighth graders would have missed the whole point. There were still students who rarely spoke and students who heard only themselves, but as a whole, my students adopted this activity and learned to share my goals, thus creating *our* discussions.

I handled my group of middle schoolers much the same way this year and only recently have tried the large group discussion with them. I am constantly amazed by their perceptions and their reactions to their peers' opinions. Without this forum, they wouldn't have access to that, so I still believe that no matter how much work or "training" it takes, it is worthwhile to have students interact in such a powerful way!

CHAPTER 15

Setting Up Classroom Routines

Elaine Perry

Elaine had always been a good organizer, but as an observant teacher candidate, she picked up many workable ideas for the classroom from her mentor teacher and other teachers she observed. Here she shares the practical ways she arranges her classroom for student success, including notebooks, grade sheets, reading aloud procedures, journals, trafficking, and the many uses of Post-it Notes. Reflecting back from her second year of teaching, Elaine explains how routines constantly evolve as teacher and students construct new learning experiences.

It is important to provide some kind of structure in the classroom to facilitate daily activities because many times the simplest of routines form a "backbone" that the students rely on from day to day. It's only logical that the activities or tasks the students will engage in on a regular basis should be systematic. When these daily practices are established and become second nature, there is more quality time left for the instructional and learning aspects of the classroom, and the routines complement or nurture these aspects.

MAKE-UP NOTEBOOK

Kathryn Bell, my supervising teacher at Jackson County High School, kept a small spiral notebook on the edge of her desk, which she referred to as the make-up book, and she expected the students to check it whenever they came back from an absence. On a daily basis, she wrote down numbers 1–5 vertically (to represent the class periods) and followed each number with a brief description of what went on and what was collected or assigned during that class. She included vocabulary lists or other detailed descriptions on the back of the page. Often she wrote, "See handout," which would prompt the students to check "slots" that she had set up above her bookcases. Each slot was labeled and represented a different class period, and contained extra copies of any handouts for absentee students.

Another teacher at Jackson County High structured her make-up work routines a little differently. She prepared a folder for each period, which contained two pockets. One side of each folder contained handouts, while the other side contained a written description of what had transpired in class. Everything was dated and the most recent material was placed on top.

Make-up work can be a teacher's worst nightmare, and although there is no method to totally eliminate the stress and irritation associated with this constant, time-consuming task, there are certain practices that can help to shift the responsibilities to the students.

GRADE SHEETS

Chanda Palmer, a ninth- and tenth-grade English teacher at Jackson County High School, created a grade sheet to be placed in front of the students' notebooks on which they could record and calculate their own grades at any given point. The "types" of grades given can serve as labels for the vertical columns. For example, there might be three columns labeled "Daily," "Writing," and "Tests." The teacher conveys what each category includes, and each time the students get a graded item back, they record the grade in the appropriate column. A formula is written below the chart to represent how the final grade is computed. For example, if daily grades, writing grades, and test grades count equally, then the formula would be: Daily Average + Writing Average + Test Average.

The grade sheets are a very detailed record of the students' progress, and learners always know where they stand. At the end of a term, the teacher can collect the sheets and compare her final figures with those calculated by the students.

READING LOGS

During a shared novel unit when students are required to read silently during class, it can be tedious for a teacher to constantly try to keep up with how quickly everyone is progressing. A simple way to record each student's quantitative progress is to require each one to keep a reading log. Some reading logs are more detailed than others, but for the most part a simple three-column chart will do. I found it helpful to have the students write the date, the reading goal, and the actual amount of reading they do. Since everyone's pace is different, it might help to add a fourth column entitled "catch-up reading."

Since the logs will be used daily, it's best to have them set up for the students to access. Since I had three classes that were using the logs, I chose to organize mine by periods in folder holders in a box located to one side of the room. The students got into the habit of passing them out daily. Usually whoever got to the room first went to the box, got them out of the appropriate folder holder, and passed them out.

It's helpful at the end of the day to be able to go through the logs and see exactly how steadily everyone is progressing and how planning should proceed from there. It's also a handy tool for the students to keep up with exactly where they are in the novel.

READING ALOUD

While observing my supervising teacher, Ms. Bell, and her classes as they read aloud, I picked up on a simple routine. She always had the students call on one another to read.

Often students do not want to read aloud in front of their peers for any number of reasons. Maybe they don't read that well and don't want to be embarrassed, or maybe they think they're just too "cool." They have a tendency to regard a teacher's calling on them as a personal vendetta to humiliate them in front of their peers. Those who do respond eagerly when a teacher calls on them to read are often pegged as a "goody-goody" or teacher's pet. Whatever their response or attitude, it's not always positive; however, when students call on students, they have no basis for the response or attitude. They can't use the excuse that the teacher is biased in some way. This routine relieves some of that pressure on the teacher and also gives the students some control.

JOURNALS

I used journals with one ninth-grade class on an everyday basis, so they needed to be organized in a system that was easily accessible to the students. I bought a large white crate and arranged three spacious folder holders in it. (I needed only three because it was a fairly small class.) Each folder holder was labeled with an alphabetical section. For example, the first held journals of students with last names falling from A–H; the next one held students with last names from I–P, and the last one held the rest. Each folder holder held approximately five or six journals, so they weren't overflowing or difficult to sort through.

I gave the students writing assignments and "picture assignments" regularly, and each student had a "form" in the front of his or her journal that provided columns to list the different assignments and due dates. This form served as a convenient checklist and grade sheet at appropriate times, and I also kept one of the forms, which I filled out with all the pertinent information, in the back of the journal crate. This was referred to as the master list and was there for the students to refer to when they had been absent.

The "picture assignments" gave the students the opportunity to draw or clip pictures that represented certain themes we were discussing in the novel. They pasted their pictures on the front of the journal folders to form a collage. In order to encourage this activity, I kept magazines and other art supplies in the room for them to utilize before or after class or at other opportune times. I had the crate set up on a small table, so the box of assorted magazines fit perfectly underneath. I kept art supplies such as labels, markers, glue, tape, stencils, and so on in a miniature crate to the side of the magazine box. This small area housed everything they would need to use on a daily basis and was organized in a way that was easy to access.

TRAFFICKING

"Trafficking" techniques may sound too mundane to even address, but when dealing with large classes (30 students or more), it's essential to have set routines for the simplest of tasks. In doing a journal project with one of my ninth-grade classes, I realized early on that collecting all of their materials daily could be very time-consuming and disorderly. They had their journals to refile, magazines or art materials to return, and copies of the novel to return to the book box. I suggested on the first day that the students on the left side of the room head to the journal area to file their journals and return materials, while I directed the students on my right to deposit their books in the box, which I placed on their side of the room. Then, they reversed directions.

Unconsciously, I continued to direct them each day after that because it just seemed orderly. Eventually, they became so used to this simple routine, they just did it on their own as I ended class each day. Such a simple routine prevented what easily could have been chaos.

POST-IT NOTES

When incorporating "visuals" or artistic assignments, it can be tedious keeping up with pictures tagged with the students' names or trying to find names written on the actual pictures. My ninth-grade advanced classes completed an ongoing bulletin board project depicting the major themes of a novel we were reading. I found that the easiest way to organize the incoming visuals and make sure that students got credit was to keep miniature post-it notes and a basket near the bulletin board. Students could quickly jot their name and an explanation of the picture (if necessary) on a post-it note, stick it on the picture, and leave the picture in the basket. I was able to give credit to the student and discard the post-it note easily and without leaving staple holes in the pictures. The basket held the pictures until the students had time to separate/group/organize the pictures for the board.

At the very least, routines maintain an orderly learning environment and encourage organizational skills. Above all, routines simply make things easier and faster for everyone. The students, as well as the teacher, become accustomed to certain practices that hold constant from day to day. In my experience, I've found that students don't resent the structure; they appreciate it. They don't feel like soldiers marching in an ordered detail or puppets responding to a cue; they realize the efficiency and ease with which some daily tasks can be handled. Establishing simple routines in the beginning and adhering to them is what makes the classroom run smoothly and almost automatically later.

REFLECTION: TWO YEARS LATER

No matter what I have ever embarked on, I have always felt the need to develop some type of organization or routine if it is needed. That's always been an innate personal attribute and one that has come in handy in teaching! Throughout student teaching, I formed routines for my students and myself to make our everyday practices run smoothly and to help us accomplish our goals.

Now, in my second year of teaching, it would be difficult for me to list or label all the many routines my eighth graders and I have set up in our classroom. To me, easy accessibility of materials like books, reading logs, or highlighters, and accurate and helpful record keeping like a "make-up workbook" or a projection calendar for upcoming library days, are simply ways of life for my students and myself.

Some routines, as just mentioned, are constants throughout the year, but other routines emerge as we begin new and different activities and we see the need for some structure. My students and the activities we do govern how my room and agenda are organized, and the students have the opportunity to give input on different routines that would be helpful.

I still believe that I have more quality time left for instruction, and they have more time for learning, when certain daily practices become second nature. I see my students improving their organizational skills and taking advantage of the structure I've established.

PART IV

Building a Collaborative Inquiry Community

The voice of the mentor teacher traditionally has been a silent one in teacher education. Although much has been written about the relationship between teacher candidates and their mentor teachers, much of the information has come from the perspective of the researcher looking *at* and not from *within* those relationships. Often in the literature on teacher education, the role of the mentor teacher is a problematic one, particularly if that role is perceived in any way to be in conflict with the "university" perpective. Our collaborative inquiry community confronted this uncomfortable issue from the very inception of the program.

Mentor teachers in this part speak frankly and openly of their feelings about how they previously had perceived and been treated by university faculty who supervised the teacher candidates in their classrooms. In Chapter 16, one mentor teacher details how long it took her to really believe in the community we were trying to build by re-envisioning this teacher education program. Chapter 17 calls for new ways of honoring and acting upon the beliefs and concerns of many mentor teachers and places in clear view the conditions necessary for true collaboration to exist between mentor teachers, university faculty, and teacher candidates.

In Chapter 18 we provide a look at how far we have come together, what we have confronted, and where we may be going. By ensuring that our work is school-based and our decisions are made for the benefit of the students in the classrooms of mentor teachers and teacher candidates, we are convinced that our work will continue and thrive in new ways. We welcome the new challenges that time and experience will bring.

CHAPTER 16

Toward an Equal Playing Field: The Role of the University Faculty from a Mentor Teacher Perspective

Chandra Adkins

Those who wonder about negotiations of power between university professors and mentor teachers in the public schools will find this chapter provocative and useful. Some mentor teachers enter into the experience with apprehension and caution born of feelings that the university regards them as "lesser" players. Chandra Adkins addresses the tension she felt initially as she confronted her perceptions of power inequities between herself and Peg Graham and Sally Hudson-Ross. Included in her discussion of those often tricky issues of power is a list of actions university personnel took that enabled her to reconceptualize both her role and the role of university professors in a field experience.

I studied at the same university with which I am now involved in the collaborative inquiry community. I student taught in another local high school that also is involved. I took courses from professors who are still at the university, and I know a great many educators who were in the profession when I first began. I shared my classroom with student teachers before I began work with this group. When I joined the collaborative inquiry community, I had many concerns that I kept voicing over and over. Primarily, all of my doubts, apprehensions, and questions centered on one thing: collaboration. Based on my background and previous experience, there were two separate entities in the supervising of teacher candidates—the role of the cooperating teacher and the role of the university professor.

When I was in the program years ago, I would be told one thing by my instructors and another, quite opposite thing by the teachers in the high school. The predominant impression was that the university offered theory that sounded good, but the reality of the high school setting was a completely

different world. I was introduced to a setting where the perception was that
teachers and teacher candidates operated together more or less independently of the way teacher candidates and the university faculty operated. As
a student teacher, I was frightened and confused by this binary polarization
and it informed what would be a lasting impression of the university personnel as kind but remote individuals who no longer understood what it meant
to be a practicing teacher. The impression of the university faculty as theore-
ticians out of touch with the reality of schools magnified when I began my
teaching career. The veterans in the building where I first began teaching
were quick to inform me that what I had learned at the university was all well
and good for a teacher education classroom but that it bore no resemblance
to what I could or should do in the "real world." I heard variations on this
theme until and during the collaborative experience I am describing currently.

When I first accepted teacher candidates into my classroom, I saw my
role as a support person for them, providing my room, my students, and an
opportunity to try out theory. When the university person came, I vanished,
believing I had no place, no role in the relationship between university and
teacher candidate. As our teacher group began meeting and the university
professors and teachers started talking about working *together,* I was suspi-
cious to say the least. Listen to my concerns in excerpts from a meeting transcript that summer.

> PEG: As you look over the project proposal, I hope it answered as
> many questions as it raised. What questions do you have? What
> did it clear up for you?
>
> ABBY: What about a journal? Are we expected to keep a journal of ev-
> erything?
>
> PEG: We do need a data trail. We hope that as we talk about different
> things you can consider in collecting data, that it's a natural add-
> on, not something new for you to do.
>
> SALLY: We hope the teacher candidate in your room helps you with
> the time issue.
>
> PEG: We hope the questions that are raised help you, are ones you are
> concerned with. It might be a different way to use a teacher candi-
> date, to inform your own teaching.
>
> BETTY [an experienced teacher researcher visiting tonight]: When you
> can make that research a part of what you do every day, when the
> journal is for you, then you keep doing it. If it's required for this
> project, then it gets to be time-consuming for you.
>
> CHANDRA: I think I'm confused.
>
> SALLY: Good, you're honest.

CHANDRA: What is the collaborative inquiry?

SALLY: [Explains her perspective on the project.]

PEG: Does that seem to be what you got in here for?

CHANDRA: I felt that I was involved in more than one thing. Teacher candidates, collaboration. . . .

PEG: It is complex.

CHANDRA: I have three more concerns: One is unique to our school. There seem to be a lot [of teachers] from other schools, and we're just two. I'm worried this could promote more divisiveness in an already divisive environment. [Discussion]

CHANDRA: Time. I know we've talked about time a lot, but I do extra-curricular, etc. I don't know when I'll do conferences. [Discussion]

CHANDRA: I'm going to reorganize my classes this year, and I'm afraid I'll look like a fool. [Discussion.]

When Peg and Sally came to my school the first week of school to meet with my colleague, Ellen Cowne (see Chapter 4), and me and our teacher candidates, we decided to take a picture of the six of us. I commented that the university people, Peg and Sally, should sit on the desktops with the remaining four of us, teachers and teacher candidates, grouped around them. This arrangement epitomized what I believed to be the hierarchical power structure that existed in our relationship.

The year started off well, but I still persisted in my belief that there were two organizational sets operating: the university and the teacher candidates, and the mentor teachers and teacher candidates. I simply did not see the whole picture of us all on the same playing field.

Even in the best of situations, problems occur. And I did have problems. My teacher candidate and I operated from quite different philosophical perspectives. These different perspectives caused me to reflect on my own practice and seriously question what I thought about teaching (see Chapter 5). When I first encountered difficulty with my situation, I said nothing. Somehow I was, if not threatened and intimidated by the university professors, under the misconception that I was inferior to them in judgment, practice, and value. I was convinced that I had no place to voice my fears and discuss my problems except with my colleague within the building. Finally, I reached a high level of frustration because talking within the building was doing nothing productive but giving me a vent outlet. I did not know what to do. Out of exasperation, but still seeing Peg and Sally as superiors, I called Peg.

What a revelation! The most comforting experience I had encountered in a long while was hearing Peg say, "I've been waiting for your call. What can we do together to work these problems through to a resolution we can all live with?" I was so shocked I wrote down on a legal pad exactly what she said and stared at it. It was one of those moments in life when you go "What?!" Then, I smiled and breathed. For the first time in months, I got it. I realized that we were in fact on the same playing field, in the same ball game, with the same goals and objectives in mind. I realized that as much as I saw myself as a facilitator within my classroom and with my teacher candidate, the university personnel were in exactly the same roles with us all. We were truly all professionals working collaboratively to achieve the same end: professional growth and education for the teacher candidate, professional growth and enrichment for the mentor teacher *and* for the university professors, and quality instruction for the students.

The university professors had established themselves as engaged in the meaning-making process with the mentors and candidates earlier in the summer when the entire mentor group began meeting. They had admitted uncertainties about the best way to proceed in providing the best possible education for the teacher candidates and had invited the mentors to share their experiences and insights in a collaborative effort to construct the most productive setting for all concerned. This is how Sally began our first meeting in May:

> We want this group to be an emerging agenda, and we have no idea, there is no program here, there is no way to do things, nobody has anything to sell, nobody has any prior commitments to anything. And in fact, we just hope that what we become as a group is something far more than any one of us could have dreamed of, I guess. It's that rare opportunity to get 25, we think, of the best teachers in the whole area to do something together over the summer and then to share what we do there with a new group of student teachers next year. . . . We're experimenting with what could happen if we really work together as a team all year long. That's the goal.

That I had not accepted the depth of their engagement is a testimony to how deeply I had internalized the earlier dichotomy of "us versus them." I don't think I've ever been more comforted as a professional educator than at the moment I realized that Peg was sincere when she asked what we could do together. I realized that she probably knew that my teacher candidate and I were struggling in our relationship, but had avoided intruding until one of us asked for her involvement.

The discussion continued with Peg and Sally taking an active role in the dialogue journal, phone calls, visits, and conferences with me and my teacher candidate. We were able, in the process, to achieve a promising relationship with valuable results for all of us. For me, the steps the university personnel took that had rewarding results were the following:

- Listening with open minds to all sides of the issue
- Setting up three- (and often four-) way conferences among mentor teacher, teacher candidate, and university instructors
- Gleaning what our different expectations were (What was I looking for that I wasn't finding with my teacher candidate? What did he need from me that I wasn't providing? What were the miscommunications between us?)
- Making contracts with everyone involved that listed clear expectations for all participants
- Participating actively in the dialogue journal
- Visiting in the school more often and observing both the mentor and the candidate while teaching
- Providing opportunities to discuss honestly and without judgment differences in opinion, philosophy, and methodology, and mediating between those differences
- Being available at all times for help and advice and listening

For the first quarter of the school year, I had hung back, reluctant to express any difficulty I was having, assuring myself that my problems were not the concerns of the university people. Their concerns, I believed, were the teacher candidates and the experience those candidates were to have. I saw Peg and Sally, at first, as superior participants with power and authority I did not have. All of the talk that had gone on in the mentor teacher meetings the summer before, talk that explained Sally and Peg as joint participants equally curious and uncertain, had meant little to me because I was choosing to continue in isolation, perceiving the university professors as threatening. I persisted in believing that to ask for help was to somehow admit weakness or incompetence (Little, 1990).

Why I persisted in that belief as long as I did had nothing to do with Peg and Sally, but everything to do with preconceived notions born out of my own experience in an empirical setting with a clear-cut chain of command. The experience I knew in dealing with persons of "rank" was the result, primarily, of teacher isolation and lack of empowerment in my own political system. Over coffee at a meeting at Peg's house during winter, I looked around and knew that I felt very comfortable with the group of fellow mentors and with Peg and Sally. I had freedom of expression, freedom to dissent and be heard, and freedom to "vent" without fear of reprisal. Still, I persisted in believing that I was not a peer until that fateful phone call with Peg. It took my willingness to accept that I did not have the answer to this problem, my willingness to act on what I believed about my security within the group and my position as an important member of the mentor group to open the door to possibility. It was the remarkable phrasing of Peg's response—the *we* of her question—that finally allowed me to accept that she and Sally did, in fact, mean what they had said all along. That one phone call, my willingness to finally make it, Peg's willingness to respond not as a person with the answers but as a person willing to work together with my candidate and me to find some acceptable choices, that was the culminating point for the prior groundwork that had been laid in our personal as well as professional relationship.

I now know what it feels like to be part of a collaborative community larger than my own building. I now accept the role of the university as a vital part of the continuing development of all teachers, and I now see myself as someone equally capable of contributing in a meaningful way to the on-going dialogue with the university, teachers across the state, and teacher candidates, as well as professionals within my own school. Peg, Sally, and Patti McWhorter had begun our project clearly dedicated to the proposition that all of us were created equals. That I hadn't understood the declaration of collaboration (see Chapter 17) was my own stumbling block, but it was an obstacle that the teacher community and, especially, the university personnel helped me to overcome.

One of the many wonderful aspects of the program, as we created it, is that many of us moved out of comfort zones into new awareness and new experiences. One teacher talked about realizing that she was uncomfortable with the way she had been conducting her discussions and the realization that they were really lectures. Another teacher revealed that she did not put her students designated as "college preparatory" into seating charts but did assign seats to those students designated as "general" ability level. It is a practice she intends to change. Another teacher talked about being excited about trying some new methods in journal writing with her classes the following year. And so it goes. Where before we may have felt isolated and afraid to ask for ideas or express shortcomings we observed in our own teaching, we now speak candidly of our failures and shortcomings and know we are still respected within the community we have built.

REFERENCE

Little, J. W. (1990). The persistence of privacy: Autonomy and initiative in teachers' professional relations. *Teachers College Record, 91*(4), 509–536.

CHAPTER 17

A Declaration of Collaboration: In a Mentor Teacher's Voice

Sally Hudson-Ross & Patti McWhorter

In 1993–94, Patti and Sally exchanged jobs as high school English teacher and university teacher educator. That shared experience led to our redesign of teacher education based on an unspoken but lived version of the declaration of collaboration below. Patti, grounded in the public middle/high school setting, brings her job exchange experience in teacher education to bear; Sally, grounded primarily in the university, speaks here from her experiences as a high school teacher during the job exchange as she worked with preservice teachers in her room. They blend their voices into one—the mentor teacher's voice—to explain what they, as teachers, wanted in a productive school/university endeavor to best educate beginning teachers. Recognizing that the teacher candidate community comprises both males and females, they have elected to use the feminine pronoun throughout—not to marginalize the men in the program but to facilitate reading of the chapter. The authors address those who plan and organize teacher education programs.

EQUALITY OF ROLES IN THE TEACHER EDUCATION PROGRAM

First of all, I am busy. My agenda and mandate are to teach my students—whether they are middle school or high school. I am committed to them and their needs. Everything else must be secondary. I care about my work and am consumed by it. I love my students, and anything that takes me away from them is difficult for me. An agenda that engages you (but not me at the moment), takes me out of my classroom, or involves someone else getting to work and play with my students is troublesome. My agenda must be central to any shared work (see Chapter 4).

You, or any observer in my classroom, cannot understand what I do until you understand the rules that govern me and my world. I answer to others—state mandates, legislation, superintendents, boards of education, administrators. I want you to understand the context in which I must make decisions. At the same time, I would welcome your help in examining and changing the constraints imposed on me. Help me to think creatively about ways to work within and around the rules that sometimes limit my thinking.

Second, I have a right to be who I am, as a person and as a teacher. My experiences, history, career stage, and current life demands make me who I am. And although I don't always say or believe this, I like who I am. I am unique and proud of my work, but I am fragile. I work in a world where everything is changing, constantly, daily, faster every year. I want to grow and be a better teacher, to be allowed to make the mistakes that come with real change. That alone qualifies me to be a strong mentor of beginning teachers. Any talk of "the best teachers" or "bad teachers" hurts deeply. On any one day, I'm both; I'll never be as good as Beth or Roger down the hall, but I'm trying. I need to know that you will not talk negatively about me or my methods once you get back in the car, back on campus, or out at another school. Do not ask me to become destabilized in front of my students, my teacher candidate, or my peers; don't push me further than I'm ready to go. As I learn, I need to maintain face, if not always control.

Third, recognize that we—university and school folks—have a history that is deep and not at all positive, whether you and I were the specific players or not. Teachers know that university people "got out" of teaching. Some think less of teachers who stayed. Others use teachers for their own gain. Teacher education faculty, in particular, seem to use graduate students for supervision, preferring to teach graduate courses rather than preservice education. Many read and write books but forget students. Others feel that time spent in schools is a waste for them professionally. It is my life they seem to reject in doing so. It's going to take time and patience on your part for me to believe that you are different. Show me in everything you do.

Fourth, as I come to trust you, I must be able to depend on you now and over the long haul. Be here when I need you, and even when I don't. Come to school, call me, return my calls. Ask (and mean it), "What's going on with your students?" and, "What do you need?" and then listen and help me if I can verbalize a need right now, or move on if I don't have time. Don't be offended, but keep asking. Let me call you at home when my teacher candidate and I have a crisis; realize that personal relationships within the small and tense space of a classroom must be smooth. If crises continue—no matter what the reasons—remove the teacher candidate. With me, my students must come first.

If my relationship with my teacher candidate fails for whatever reason, keep me in the mentor teacher group; don't let me lose my connections when

I need them most. And please, make a long-term commitment to our group. Don't invent a program and then turn it over to someone else; don't rotate leaders every year so we have to learn to trust again; don't abandon us when a better idea comes along. We need continuity—we crave it.

Fifth, find the humility it takes to be a co-learner and friend with me. Examine your own practice and program, question the research and theory you espouse, sponsor and come to "happy hours" and parties, introduce me to your peers as your friend (not one of "our" teachers), help me find new ways to grow and become more of a professional, and, most of all, trust me too.

COLLABORATION AND CO-RESEARCH

For all my not wanting to leave my classroom, I have been alone in here too long. A teacher candidate who shares my room and students all year can be a partner, a friend, a second parent even, who cares about them as much as I do, who struggles with how to make things work better. I don't have enough time to talk to every student, to analyze surveys, to see what is affecting students' lives outside my classes, as much as I'd like to. But a teacher candidate conducting her own research (see chapters in Part II) to learn about students—interviewing writers and their writing, examining their attitudes toward reading literature at home and school, shadowing a student through the school day—can summarize and bring that information to me in a format I can survey quickly. She also can raise questions that I, in the daily routine of things, cannot see:

- Why *do* I do make-up work this way—what are other options?
- Why are students so bored with these short stories?
- Why do the boys in our room always act out but the girls stay quiet?
- Why are they failing my tests?
- What will happen if we give them more choices for what they read or write?

Together, we can explore shared questions—our real questions, not ones imposed from outside—in informal ways throughout the year. With two of us, we can manage short taped interviews, collecting and analyzing questionnaires, keeping focused notes in a dialogue journal as one of us observes the other, focusing on one struggling student's growth. The teacher candidate partner can bring me insights from her peers in other schools who share what they learn from other mentors. They can share their papers and Think Pieces and journals on reading new texts, allowing me to enter into a professional dialogue when I don't have time to do the reading or take a class. From this perspective, a teacher candidate gives me what only university professors have had: a research assistant!

Together, having learned what we sought, we can move on to new questions that emerge, to new experiments, to sometimes sharing with other teachers and learning with them in the professional arena. What I get is staff development tailored to my classroom, housed, in fact, in my space. For once, I don't have to go downtown to learn something. What my teacher candidate gets is a setting for inquiry, for experimenting with me and alone, for developing a research mind-set that I hope will always lead her to both ask questions and seek partners with whom to teach and grow. We do *not* have to be alone.

Although I don't care whether teacher candidates "physically" meet in our school for their college courses, I do respect their need to learn outside the middle or high school classroom as well. They need and deserve time to read texts and to explore issues with their peers who are in the same beginning place. However, the "mental" location of that campus work should be in my classroom and the classrooms of the other mentor teachers in our group. If teacher candidates read a book, they should decide on its credibility just as I do—as a measure of how it makes sense with my students. If they analyze data across schools, they should be aware of individual and group differences as well. They must learn the teacher's realistic way of assessing the reliability and current value of research, theory, and other literature in the field. First of all it must be adaptable to my setting.

Those who teach campus courses must realize that teaching and English/language arts are fully integrated for me: in theory and practice, in discipline and planning and building community, in composition and language and literature. In my life, I cannot separate out issues of multiple intelligence, cooperative learning, crisis management, or reader response. University people who see these as separate courses, units, or lines of research make my job look easier than it is. Instead, a teaching life is constantly in flux, constantly moving and full of impromptu decisions; it is both complex and of the moment. Campus courses must reflect that truth and deal with teacher candidates' issues as they emerge. As a result, college teachers must be willing to learn with their students just as I do. They too must be researchers in their own classrooms, model the behaviors we expect of new and experienced teachers, and join all of us in creating new visions of teaching and learning.

MULTIPLE, INTERRELATED COMMUNITIES OF LEARNERS

If in this age we believe that knowledge is constructed socially through the interactions of two or more people, if we want our students to learn through

Mentor teacher Fran Bullock *(standing)* co-teaches a campus class of 1998 teacher candidates. *Seated in foreground, left to right,* Fran's teacher candidate, Amy Moore, and class colleagues Jennifer Heeder and Stephen Castile.

discussions and engagement with the insights of others, then we too deserve opportunities to learn with our peers. A group founded on collaborative and collegial inquiry and growth means that I belong in many ways, that I am invited to become more of myself and enjoy my work. Interrelated communities of learners provide the forum for meaningful and rewarding professional growth.

Mentor Teacher and Teacher Candidate

When a teacher candidate is in my classroom all year, we develop a relationship far deeper than short-term student teaching allows. I know; I've had student teachers or been one myself. Traditionally I am asked to turn over my students to a young stranger, perhaps after a brief observation period. My administrators and I worry about the quality of education our students are getting, about the difficulties we will encounter and have to solve, about how to provide advice without offending—our time is so short! A teacher candidate in that setting must read and plan, get to know students and school, walk the tense line of friendship with a mentor teacher she has met only recently, balance campus seminars, and, through it all, be evaluated. And we wonder why the first year of teaching is so tough.

Instead, realize that relationships take time to build. Tensions are normal, but as in any relationship, they can be resolved over time and experience and coming to know one another as people. With an ongoing, shared focus on our students, neither the teacher candidate nor I need to fear the insecurity of hasty, evaluative judgments. (Yes, they judge us too!) Instead of concern for ourselves, our attention is constantly pulled back to the students. Through written dialogue journals we present, question, and argue the tough issues that sometimes we cannot speak.

Being a teacher educator or mentor—not a supervising teacher of student teaching—gives me perspective; I *know* this person whom I'm able to coach and struggle with through an entire year. It allows me to trust her gradually as I watch her learn to know and understand my students, to manage their behaviors for learning, to become a part of my school, to plan for our situation, and to teach little by little by little. When it is her turn, I am excited to watch my newest peer fly on her own, knowing that my students are safe. I expect her first year to be smooth (barring irrational job demands) because I know she now has the skills to make her own way, to create her own communities of learners.

Mentor Teacher and University Teacher Group

But I too need my care and feeding. It is tough to work through the issues of a new teacher candidate every year, tough to learn this much at once, and I don't want to do it alone.

First, I want to feel ownership and power over the teacher education program as a whole. I want to be involved in making placements, and to speak out about assignments, expectations of teacher candidates in my room and school, and program development. I want to be sure that neither my teacher candidate nor I are put in uncomfortable situations or put through worthless hoops. Meeting in a small group with representative mentors from other schools and the university teachers allows me to hear how others feel and to help us compromise to meet everyone's needs. In whole group meetings I can see how my situation is just like everyone else's (what a relief) or truly unique (and ask for special help if needed). As we continually negotiate the program, I know it is mine.

From my mentor teacher group I want several things: sympathy (lots of it), food and friendship, laughter, chances to travel and get attention for my good work, freedom from my isolation, a refuge in these difficult times, intellectual stimulation connected directly to my classroom and school. The individual power of each mentor teacher grows in our gatherings; together we create strength. Because our focus is always on the teacher candidates and our students, I do not feel that I am being judged. Instead, this is a place where we all experiment and learn. The group moves me forward.

My own department is enriched by our experiences outside the school. We bring new ideas and insights and problems from our discussions with other mentor teachers, and we continue those discussions in our own workroom. Cross-school visitations empower me to see in new ways what a text or talk never can. If I am one of only two or three in my department, or our department is the only one in the school that wants to think deeply about teaching, we gain a cohort of similar peers through the collaborative inquiry group. If our department or school is strong, we get to share with others what we've learned locally. Time is hard to come by—always—but time spent with mentor teacher peers enriches me and my setting as no other professional activity can.

Teacher Candidate and Peer University Group

I'm glad my teacher candidate has her own peers to rely on and to learn with. To be honest, it takes some of the burden off me because I know she is cared for by so many others. Besides, I know that she has interests, questions, problems (even tensions with me) that I've grown beyond but that other beginners need to struggle with. Her teacher candidate group also has a year to gel as a community of learners—they read together, compare research findings across schools, debate and discuss, read and respond to each other's Think Pieces and portfolios, share teacher talk and stories. As I have come to value my peers more and more at this point in my career, I believe it is essential that she too know the value of a community for her own personal sanity and growth as a teacher. I hope that my peers and I show her in everything we do that strong professional and personal relationships with colleagues matter, and that we help her know how to find like-minded partners in her future.

Being with one teacher all year allows a special bond, a special opportunity to know students as they develop. This means, however, that my teacher candidate experiences only one school in depth. Luckily, her peers are placed in several other middle and high schools, they teach students from a range of circumstances from rural to suburban to urban, they encounter problems my school doesn't, and they share how their mentor teachers do things differently than I do. She gets the opportunity to visit her peers in their schools, to see their students on video, and to talk about their varied experiences. Thus, although she may not experience each setting, she is aware of a broader range of possibilities while enjoying the benefits of a year-long, stable situation.

Through her teacher candidate group, she also becomes a part of the larger profession by reading professional journals, presenting her research and listening to that of others at conferences, listening to a range of speakers from our group and beyond, and staying abreast of current issues, theories, research, and methods. I envy her her time to reflect so much (and know she doesn't yet realize *why* that time is so special), but I hope that by coming to think this deeply now, she will always see teaching as a learning process.

Mentor Teachers and University Teachers

I am on a first-name basis with my university colleagues; I know they care about my students—meet with us, party with us, cry with us, grow themselves as part of our multiple communities. They accept leadership for making things happen that mentor teachers cannot: They set up meetings, arrange for food, find funding for us to travel and to do our work, bring us resources, listen. But they, too, need their own rewards.

I understand that I may not see university faculty for weeks at a time when they need to write or teach another course. Yet I know that their hearts are with those of us in the schools, that they like being here, that they want to be with us—and that they will sneak out when they can just for fun. When two of them team teach, they support both us and each other. They can alternate who is teaching on campus and who is visiting. They can spell each other for writing or conference time. One of them is always available by phone or can be available in an emergency. Together, the two or three of them create a team—just like my teacher candidate and me—that can explore their own teaching, share their own students (the teacher candidates and, I suppose, us too), conduct research about how we all learn and grow together, publish it with and for us to let others understand what we have discovered. It is possible and acceptable for us all to earn our respective rewards of value within our very different worlds.

In her presidential address to the American Educational Research Association, Ann Lieberman (1992) called for the kind of work we are conducting. Collaborative work in schools/universities, she said, will produce new knowledge that

> cannot be categorized as basic or applied research; it is knowledge that is co-constructed and owned by practitioner and researcher alike. . . . They are scholars and they are advocates for transforming schools. They are creators of knowledge and critical analysts of the change process. . . . The practice–theory connection is no better served than when it is lived. We can learn *from* as well as *about* practice. Our challenge is to create a community that educates all of us, those in the university and those in the schools, a community that expands our relationships with one another and, in so doing, our knowledge and our effectiveness. (pp. 10–11)

In my experiences, I have found that simple conversations can be the beginning of powerful relationships and the kinds of communities Lieberman described. I hope others will join us in confronting and overcoming the barriers that have kept us apart. Our students, after all, will be the ultimate winners.

REFERENCE

Lieberman, A. (1992). The meaning of scholarly activity and the building of community (presidential address at the annual meeting of the American Educational Research Association, April 1992). *Educational Researcher, 21*(6), 5–12.

CHAPTER 18

Retrospective

Peg Graham, Sally Hudson-Ross, Chandra Adkins, Patti McWhorter, & Jennifer McDuffie Stewart

The preceding chapters articulated the beginnings of the collaborative inquiry group and described the many different components of our experiences. In this chapter, the editors narrow the lens and focus on issues of co-reform and collaborative inquiry as the theoretical framework for the shared professional development of mentor teachers and university professors. This retrospective look is based on analyses of extensive data across 4 years, including weekly bulletins, transcribed interviews with participants, dialogue journals, field notes, class assignments, projects, and products. In particular, we use these data to explore the following questions: How have we grown and changed as a group? What are the foundations of this collaborative inquiry community as it moves into its fifth year?

BACKGROUND AND DEVELOPMENT: HOW HAVE WE GROWN AND CHANGED AS A GROUP?

Collaborations among mentor teachers and university professors have focused on three themes across our 4 years together: teacher education, school–department–teacher change, and relationships. The first year can be summarized as *beginning*. Mentor teachers and university professors created a new vision, calendar, assignments, and principles for teacher education based on a concept of teacher research. Team teaching in both school and campus classrooms forced everyone to raise questions, articulate beliefs, and collaborate across settings. As a result of careful negotiation and conscious support for one another's worlds, the group built trust, established patterns for communication, and explored how we could renegotiate power relationships.

In the second year, we focused on *refining* what we had built. We used the feedback of all participants—now including graduates—to make explicit teacher candidates' campus and school experiences, to develop assessment tools, and to create and grow comfortable with routines for ongoing collaboration. Mentors became more confident in their new roles and with teacher research. They began to engage as group members in professional development activities both locally and across the state and nation and to nominate and support new mentors in their own schools.

By the third year, we *experimented with extending* the model of a collaborative inquiry community of mentor teachers and university professors to include all 50 preservice teachers in English education. We learned that other university colleagues perceived the model to be prohibitively time-consuming and to take them away from research interests. As a result, we returned to our original cadre of two professors and 30 mentor teachers, more aware of the complexities involved in trying to replicate a collaborative inquiry group such as ours. We recognized—as have many professional development school leaders—that those who enjoy this work perceive ongoing collegial sites as the foundation of their scholarship, broadly defined to combine teaching, research, and service. In the meantime, many mentor teachers in the new schools appreciated the school/university relationships and experienced the excitement of challenging their own teaching with teacher candidates and university colleagues in a year-long experience. Experienced mentors felt rewarded for leadership roles among mentors, for publications they had participated in, and for knowledge and skills they realized they had acquired.

In the fourth year, the group needed a period of *stabilization* to re-examine routines, assignments, projects, and goals. During the summer of 1997, group members were also more ready to turn to *self-reflection* in order to examine our own practice and student learning more carefully. We focused the summer agenda on the National Council of Teachers of English standards for English/language arts, and three groups explored block scheduling curriculum (a pressing issue for most), student assessment, and mentoring. As the group gained coherence, this year also provided multiple and diverse opportunities for professional development through presentations and publications and statewide and national committees and development teams.

At the same time, intensive collaboration and communication across 4 years have led us to new awareness of and involvement in the local tensions within each department—both school and university. Mentor teachers are tired after 4 years of full-time partners in their schools, but are concerned about varying levels of buy-in among their peers, including those who came on board later with less engagement in the group. Circumstances have set up the year ahead to force us to renegotiate at an important time in the development of the group. As most schools move to block scheduling, the university will convert from quarters to semesters, requiring us to re-examine every phase of our shared work as well as how we work within our own sites. At this extraordinarily busy and demanding time of change, we perceive the group to be strong enough to make wise decisions to carry us all into a new phase. Grounding us all in a commitment to continue is informal feedback from graduates and their administrators who report successes of first- through third-year teachers. While only 53% of teacher education graduates teach in Georgia in the year following graduation (Georgia Partnership for Excellence in Education, 1997), our hiring rates have been 95% (1995, with 20 students), 70% (1996, with 20 students), and 67% (1997, with 48 students). Initial, formal data from surveys and interviews suggest that graduates have found career success and are staying in teaching at rates higher than state averages.

PROFESSIONAL DEVELOPMENT IN ONE COLLABORATIVE INQUIRY COMMUNITY

In order to see how far we have come, it is important to re-examine who we were in 1994 when we first came together. Peg and Sally, as university professors, recently had been involved in schools as public school teachers in 1994, and Patti had just taught a year on campus. Their initial goals were to develop a teacher education program that recognized, celebrated, and explored the realities of classroom experience while grounding that experience in current research and theory. At the same time, mentor teachers-to-be listed four major categories of reasons for agreeing to participate in a school/university collaboration:

- *University-related reasons.* To stay in touch with university faculty or to someday go into teacher education or supervision themselves
- *Department-related reasons.* To work more collegially and professionally with their own colleagues, reduce their isolation, and help the department get out of "ruts"
- *Commitment to teacher preparation.* To help student teachers, learn from them, and improve on their own experience throughout student teaching
- *Reflective practice.* To think about their own teaching

When asked to articulate questions they had about their own practice, many mentors had difficulty in 1994. In retrospect, those who did generate questions continue to explore the same issues in 1998: challenging students to work at deeper levels, traditional versus more progressive teaching strategies, assessment, reaching all students, coverage versus depth, and becoming a more inspired and inspiring teacher. In many ways, these career-long questions pervade the discussions of the group now, moving a single teacher's concern to the realm of professional dialogue. Interestingly, the same questions fit the university professors' world view with their own students— the teacher candidates. Peg and Sally, as team teachers themselves across all coursework and student teaching, find that collaboration both within a classroom and across teaching sites is a blessing for their own very active, reflective practice.

By May 1995, the end of the collaborative inquiry group's first year, mentor teachers' goals had been met and new iterations of their questions emerged—now more collaboratively voiced. When asked to write "How have you grown personally this year as an English teacher and participant in this project?" teachers overwhelmingly reported four categories of responses:

- *Challenge.* The experience challenged practice, standards for students, and the ability to articulate, to raise questions, to think more broadly, to engage in research, and to stay open-minded.
- *Collaboration.* The experience led teachers to value interactions with cross-school and within-school peers, to build a support network, to decrease isolation, to perceive they were not alone in their problems, and to feel valued by university partners.
- *Being a teacher educator.* The year-long collaboration with a teacher candidate encouraged teaming, better mentoring, and willingness to "give up" classes and students to a young professional.
- *Renewal.* Many mentors claimed pivotal growth experiences ("It all came together for me this year"), a new level of professional engagement, confidence, a peace and stability in their work, and a refreshing outlook on teaching and English.

Mentors' new goals included research, further learning, reflection, time to enjoy teaching more, more writing, and better mentoring. New concerns included comparing a new teacher candidate with a previous one and the age-old issue of time for family and one's own life.

Teachers also reported an impact of the collaboration on the work of their local school departments. They perceived that their departments were more open, connected, communicative, sharing, and interested in one another's work. They felt they had more time to share and learn together as well as to celebrate successes and struggle with problems. Many mentors suggested that teacher candidates were more than just student teachers; instead, they had become involved in departmental and school life. These departmental findings did not hold for all, however. For example, some mentors felt segregated or elitist; in one case, both mentors left the school in the following year due to school issues unrelated to the collaborative inquiry group. Working within the complex realities of public schools, we realize that very real issues of local tensions continue to exist and must be respected as part of the professional dialogue. The collaborative group, in our case, provided a springboard for one mentor to enter graduate school and another to feel supported in a time of local criticism.

Shared work within a collaborative inquiry community across schools requires careful handling of usually hidden problems. We spent much of our first years learning how to deal with local school issues respectfully, how to take problems to the group for examination and solutions, how to negotiate tensions among participants (teacher candidate and mentor, teacher candidates as a group, mentor teachers within a school, etc.), and how to elevate the overall work to a professional level. Like the mentor teachers, Peg and Sally were often exhausted in the daily enactment of the work but were equally energized by the results they saw in teacher candidate and student learning, the group's evolution, and their own practice as teachers and researchers.

WHERE WE ARE NOW: THE FOUNDATIONS OF A COLLABORATIVE INQUIRY COMMUNITY IN ITS FOURTH YEAR

As we move into Year 5 of our collaborative inquiry community—now with our own acronym UGA–NETS (for University of Georgia Network for English Teachers and Students), we are aware of the need to restructure our project's design due to block scheduling and university semester conversion. But before we can move forward, we are keenly aware of the need to reflect on two questions: What are the foundations of this collaborative inquiry community in its fourth year? What are the missteps and tensions we are aware of as we identify those foundational elements? We ask the former question in an effort to determine what works within our community, and the latter question in an effort to examine our weaknesses. In reflecting on those questions, we have identified three areas that constitute the cornerstones of our shared work: cultural norms, communication, and professional springboards.

Cultural Norms

Patterns of group interaction, collaboration, and expectations over the past 4 years have evolved into a set of cultural norms we are able to identify with UGA–NETS. Teachers and professors participate actively in the group. That is, they are not members in name only, but assume responsibility for establishing summer agendas, actively mentoring teacher candidates, and taking on leadership roles in a variety of ways. Criteria for selecting new members call for teachers who are "growing" and questioning. This aspect of our culture certainly could be viewed as exclusive rather than inclusive. And that, admittedly, has led to tensions for some departments and individuals who would include any teacher willing to welcome a student teacher into her classroom. For those who have long participated in the group, the norm is to move away from completely open membership in favor of identifying those who seek to develop professionally.

One of the reasons for selecting participants carefully is the cultural imperative that participants in UGA–NETS assume a teacher researcher stance. A central principle of our shared work has been to cultivate a greater comfort with the idea of uncertainty. Whereas teachers often are placed in situations by those outside of teaching to claim certainty, stability, and confidence in their decision making, our group has begun to realize how often suspending closure on what works is the better path. But embracing uncertainty does not mean a teacher must merely guess about how and what to teach. Instead, we would ask one another to continually pose questions and use the research tools we have begun to assemble in order to make better decisions as teachers. Teacher research as a way of knowing provides an alternative for teacher candidates who would seek right answers and recipes from mentors and university faculty rather than struggle with the complex problems they encounter in schools and classrooms. But intentional and systematic inquiry takes time and patience. Despite the new tensions that can arise from assuming a teacher researcher stance, the group as a whole is fully committed to this aspect of our community.

A central norm growing from sustained efforts to cultivate a teacher research mind-set is that group members seek to better understand the different sociocultural and political contexts in which we all work. Sensitive to our different local contexts, we also appreciate how members have cultivated different kinds of expertise and ways of knowing. As a result, mentors emerge not only as knowledgeable peers to university faculty—who historically have been assigned a more privileged position in the educational hierarchy—but often as their superiors. Others in the group aspire to leadership positions and feel rewarded by opportunities for public recognition of their expertise. Of course, the question of power and recognition for members is also rife with tension. Is it possible for current leaders—teachers and professors alike—to share those roles and encourage others to aspire to leadership positions? And, if not, can we continue to flourish as a collaborative inquiry community?

The constant push to realign roles and cultivate close working relationships between school- and campus-based colleagues has resulted in greater trust among constituents. A prime example of that occurred this year as we shuffled four teacher candidates from one placement to another. Based on input from both teacher candidates and mentor teachers, those of us on campus deemed it necessary to rearrange placements (see Chapter 17). Although this is the largest number of changes we have ever made, the mentor teacher group fully appreciates the range of tensions, both personal and professional, that can lead to a problematic teacher candidate/mentor teacher working relationship. Whereas mentor teachers might have considered themselves a failure if their teacher candidate was reassigned in the past, our shared history and experiences with placement issues have altered that attitude. Mentors have trusted campus colleagues to make these changes as long as the change is the result of close negotiations with all those directly involved. This attitude has been possible to foster due to the second cornerstone of our group: communication.

Communication

Across 4 years, we have fostered closer communication by developing more avenues for talk and opportunities for every member to initiate dialogue. The single most important communication tool has been the weekly bulletin published by the campus teachers. If mentors are to support what unfolds in the campus classroom, they need to know exactly what is being studied and when. Weekly bulletins contain the goals, activities, and assignments for the week as well as a preview of the upcoming week. Each of the participating departments has a set of the campus texts so mentors have access to what their teacher candidates are studying. This allows mentors to consider the teacher candidates' work load and assist them in becoming better time managers. In addition, the bulletin offers mentors news about the group—professional development opportunities, upcoming conferences and meetings, updates on projects, and personal notes about members who have had babies, surgery, or the like.

Each mentor teacher and teacher candidate pair also keeps a dialogue journal (see Chapter 3). Campus faculty write in the dialogue journals weekly, allowing them a glimpse into the pair's shared practice in the schools. Here, the mentor and teacher candidate can address tensions more safely since the dialogue journal offers distance and an opportunity to think before responding to inquiries and constructive critiques. Likewise, it provides a site for school-based and university-based colleagues to disagree or question one another productively. We have found that differences, when voiced by caring professionals, allow teacher candidates to appreciate multiple perspectives on complex issues of teaching and learning rather than assume that a single "right" answer is possible. The dialogue journal has emerged as an extremely important communication tool.

A number of mentor teacher/teacher candidate pairs maintain dialogue journals via electronic mail. All participants in UGA–NETS have an e-mail account through the university, which has streamlined communication efforts for all. Through e-mail and phone calls, we have managed to support a communication network that provides immediate response, intervention, or information for those members who would seek it. As trust has been fostered in the group, communications have expanded dramatically. Mentor teachers know that our work with teacher candidates is a collaborative effort in which all of us are teacher educators working toward common goals. We have all learned the importance of sharing those data in order to better serve teacher candidates' needs as learners and emerging professionals. Moreover, with 4 years and multiple cases of past teacher candidates from which to work, we do a much better job of detecting patterns of tension and issues of concern to the preservice teachers. And we have begun to see those tensions as sites of inquiry rather than problems to be avoided or ignored.

Communication efforts also have been fostered by school visits. Campus colleagues make an effort to be visible in the schools, which has been helpful in establishing a context for more effective communications, but those visits also have made university faculty aware of the need to inform building administrators about the work mentors do. Administrators are more likely to recognize the contributions mentors are making to the teaching profession when they have a full understanding of what that work entails and how it contributes to a teacher's own professional development. Thus, university colleagues update building administrators about the group's activities and invite administrators to participate in activities such as the 1997 Georgia Partnership for Excellence in Education Bus Stop. At the Bus Stop presentation, administrators participated in focus group discussions with mentors, graduates, and teacher candidates, and had the chance to listen to their own teachers present findings about the group's work. In addition, UGA–NETS leaders (department chairs, committee chairs, university professors) write letters and talk individually with administrators in order to secure permission for teacher candidates and their mentors to collect data for teacher research projects and for mentor teachers to participate in conference presentations and other professional development opportunities.

As much promise as all of these lines of communication hold, communications are still tricky sometimes. The most difficult problem seems to center on professional development opportunities. Some teachers appear to need more than one "invitation." That is, an announcement in the bulletin about a chance to present at a national conference, for example, may interest a teacher, but she also may feel the need for a more personalized invitation to join in the activity. Those second invitations are time-consuming, but have proved necessary for those teachers who feel less confident about the expertise they may bring to the endeavor or are simply more tentative than other members.

Professional Springboards

The role of creating opportunities for mentors to grow by extending their reach beyond the classroom has been assumed by the university faculty. They have fed information to teachers and sought grants to support an array of professional development initiatives. Because university colleagues have assumed the bulk of responsibility for disseminating information about professional development opportunities and for recruiting participants, they have also sought to encourage mentor teachers to "raise the bar" on expectations for the group.

One way to do that is by sponsoring large group summer seminars where participants negotiate the agenda for reading and study across the summer, based on their current needs and interests. Here, expertise developed elsewhere is elaborated as the group provides a venue for sharing and connected knowing through sustained dialogue. Because interests across the group are wide-ranging, university colleagues have begun to peel off in different directions to feed their own special areas of interest. For example, Sally has initiated a project with a professor in the English department to explore how the program in Arts and Sciences and Education connect. Together, the two professors support a listserv for current teacher candidates, mentor teachers, and graduates to talk about their preparation as teachers. Peg has organized a team of teachers to function as the External Development Team for the Adolescent and Young Adult/English Language Arts (AYA/ELA) National Board for Professional Teaching Standards (NBPTS) certificate. Teachers try out the portfolio exercises, provide input to the test developers, and support pilot participants for the assessment. Through participation in these and other activities, UGA–NETS is beginning to raise the bar across its collaborative efforts.

However, lest we become too complacent, it is important to point out the missteps we experience in our efforts to provide professional springboards for everyone. As mentioned previously, some mentors may assume the existence of an "inner circle" of teachers who are more knowledgeable or more talented than others. It is certainly true that some people volunteer more and consistently assume leadership positions. For that reason, we do seek to offer special encouragement to some mentors to participate, and we issue a second or third invitation to those who are most tentative. In other cases, we have devised professional development opportunities that will showcase the expertise of a particular group of teachers. Our collaborative inquiry group is also aware that some participants may have reached a "plateau," which requires all of us to experiment with ways to challenge one another to move and grow. UGA–NETS has approached that dilemma in a number of ways. One is through the collaborative community's seminars and the questions and reflective comments offered by other mentor teachers. A second, equally powerful, way is through the questions posed by teacher candidates as they observe in classrooms (school *and* university) and seek the reasons for teachers' decisions. Their questions tend to be genuine and require clearly articulated rationales from their mentor teachers and professors.

Whatever we do as a collaborative inquiry group, though, we must continue to remind ourselves that participants join the group with widely different levels of buy-in. We all have varied growth patterns that depend on personal as well as professional situations, and we all work in contexts and cultures that impede or accelerate growth. Thus, the complexity of a group such as ours means that we can expect few simple answers to resolving the tensions we identify. However, by the end of this fourth year of our project, we think we have created a context that is more amenable to growth, change, challenge, and risk taking. We build on the knowledge that our group provides a space of relative safety to be uncertain and a mutual support system for school and university colleagues.

REFERENCE

Georgia Partnership for Excellence in Education. (1997). *Columbia Group index of teachers and teaching.* Atlanta: Author.

Front row, left to right, Peg Graham, Patti McWhorter, Sally Hudson-Ross, Ginny Speaks James, Beth Tatum, and Barbara Jarrard. *Middle row,* Lillian Chandler, Mindi Rhoades, Jennifer McDuffie Stewart, Christina Healan, Jerelyn Wallace, and Jeff Anderson. *Back row,* Buddy Wiltcher, Elaine Perry, Amy Wilbourne, Chandra Adkins, and Roger Bailey.

About the Editors and the Contributors

EDITOR-CONTRIBUTORS

Peg Graham co-teaches with Sally Hudson-Ross in the Language Education Department at the University of Georgia. Peg taught high school for 17 years in Iowa and received her B. A., M. A., and Ph.D. from the University of Iowa. She is an assessment designer for the National Board for Professional Teaching Standards, is an active member of NCTE Conference on English Education (CEE) committees, and is interested in school/university collaborations, mentoring, and professional development in English. Recently she has published articles in *English Education, English Journal,* and *Teaching and Teacher Education.* In 1997, Peg received the Russell Undergraduate Teaching Award, an honor granted to the best teachers at UGA.

Sally Hudson-Ross co-teaches with Peg Graham in the Language Education Department at the University of Georgia. Sally taught high school in Ohio and Georgia, served as Language Arts Consultant K–12 in Gwinnett County, Georgia, and after earning her Ph.D. from the University of Georgia, taught at the University of Northern Iowa before returning to the faculty of UGA in 1987. During the 1993–94 school year, Sally and Patti McWhorter exchanged jobs for a year, a life-changing event. Sally serves as Co-Reform Chair for the UGA College of Education and is involved in state co-reform efforts. She served as Local Arrangements Chair for NCTE in Atlanta and is a member of CEE committees. Sally's current interests are school/university collaborations and professional development in English, and she has published in *English Journal, English Education, Reading Teacher,* and *Research in the Teaching of English* and co-edited *Children's Voices,* published by Heinemann.

Chandra Adkins, who has earned a B.S.Ed., M.Ed., and Ph.D. from UGA, was a mentor teacher at Washington-Wilkes High School during the first year of our collaboration. As a full-time student from 1995 to 1998, Chandra team-taught with Peg and Sally on campus while co-editing this book. She completed her Ph.D. in 1998 and chose to continue her investigations of adolescent literature and gender, race, and class inequities as an English teacher at Washinton-Wilkes High School. During her teaching years, she earned the Dedicated Teacher Award; at UGA, she won the Louise McBee Scholarship and Outstanding Teaching Assistant Award; and her paper on presentism in adolescent literature, her dissertation, was a highlighted session at AERA in 1998.

184 ABOUT THE EDITORS AND THE CONTRIBUTORS

Patti McWhorter teaches English and is department chair at Cedar Shoals High School, where she has taught for 17 years. She earned her B.S.Ed., M.Ed., and Ph.D. in the Language Education Department at UGA and taught there full time during 1993–94 in a job exchange with Sally Hudson-Ross. She is an adjunct professor for Piedmont College in Athens and conducts inservice workshops across the state. Patti has been named GCTE Teacher of the Year and GATE Supervising Teacher of the Year, served on the CEE nominating committee and NCTE Local Arrangements Committee in Atlanta, and led her department as members in the School Research Consortium of the National Reading Research Center. A constant teacher researcher, Patti's current interests are active learning, student-centered classrooms, and standards/assessment.

Jennifer McDuffie Stewart teaches English at Habersham Central High School in Mount Airy, Georgia. She received a B.S.Ed. from the University of Georgia and is currently working on an M.Ed., also at UGA. She currently is researching to find out more about the reading habits of high school students.

CONTRIBUTORS

Jeff Anderson teaches English at Lovejoy High School in Clayton County. He received a B.S.Ed. from the University of Georgia and is currently working on an M.Ed. at West Georgia.

Susanna Blackstone is an English teacher at Clarke Central High School in Athens, Georgia. She has received both a B. A. and an M.Ed. from the University of Georgia and is interested in research regarding classroom management.

Lillian Chandler teaches English at Madison County High School, where she is also department chair. She received both a B.S.Ed. and an M.Ed. from the University of Georgia and has been chosen as Star Teacher at her school.

Ellen Cowne is the assistant principal at Henderson Middle School in Jackson, Georgia. She taught English for 25 years and has received numerous honors, including being chosen as GCTE Teacher of the Year and Star Teacher at her school on seven different occasions. She also has had a poem published in *English Journal* and several articles published in *Connections*.

Jennifer Dail teaches language arts at Saint John the Evangelist Catholic School in Hapeville, Georgia. She obtained a B.S.Ed. from the University of Georgia and currently is researching various writing issues in the classroom.

Cheryl Protin Hancock earned her B.S.Ed. from UGA and is currently a freelance writer, wife, and mother of two children. She has published articles in *Athens Magazine* and written two career books with Learning Express.

Her current interests are children's books and adolescent literature, especially what children like in books and what they learn from reading.

Katherine Hatcher teaches English at Mount de Sales Academy in Macon, Georgia. She received a B.S.Ed. from the University of Georgia.

Christina Healan is an English teacher at Jackson County Comprehensive High School in Jefferson, Georgia. She received a B.A. and M.Ed. from the University of Georgia and currently is conducting research to determine what motivates students to stay in school.

Amy Ragland Ingalls teaches language arts at Hilsman Middle School in Athens, Georgia. She received a B.S.Ed. from the University of Georgia and is researching cooperative group learning and student-generated curriculum at the middle-grade level.

Heather Ivester is completing her A. B. degree in Japanese and raising two children as a wife, homemaker, and freelance writer in Athens, Georgia. Her B. A. in English is from Auburn University and her M.Ed. from UGA. She also has taught English as a Second Language in Japan and worked as a proofreader. Her current interests are ESL and child development.

Andrea Bottoms Jacobson teaches at Milton High School in Alpharetta, Fulton County, Georgia. She earned her B.A. in English and M.Ed. in English education, both from UGA. She currently is teaching juniors and seniors and is especially interested in implementing the College Board Pacesetter Program.

Ginny Speaks James teaches English at Centennial High School in Roswell, Georgia. She received a B.A. and an M.Ed. from the University of Georgia and is interested in researching ways in which to teach and assess writing.

Gretchen King earned her B.S.Ed. from UGA and has been teaching at Gordon Central High School in Calhoun, Georgia.

Amy Ledvinka received a B.S.Ed. from the University of Georgia. She is interested in researching motivation among students.

Susan Little teaches English at Clarke Central High School in Athens, Georgia. She has taught for 25 years, has been chosen Teacher of the Year, and is interested in researching aspects of literacy. Most recently, she received a six-year degree from Alabama–Birmingham University.

Erin McDermott completed her MAT in Teaching English to Speakers of Other Languages (TESOL) at the Monterrey Institute of International Studies in California in 1998. She earned her B.S.Ed. from UGA.

Margie Michael taught English at Madison County High School in Danielsville, Georgia, for 12 years. She was a founding member of the UGA–NETS group. Margie passed away in 1996. Her son, Sean, graduated from the program that same year and is teaching English at George Walton Academy in Monroe, Georgia.

Elaine Perry teaches language arts at Creekland Middle School in Lawrenceville, Georgia. She received a B.S.Ed. from the University of Georgia and currently is researching how to teach the writing process to students.

Mindi Rhoades teaches English at Cedar Shoals High School in Athens, Georgia. She received a B.A. and an M.Ed. from the University of Georgia and is interested in researching student-centered classrooms. She also has had an NRRC publication.

Greg Slattery is an English teacher at Oconee County High School in Watkinsville, Georgia. He received an A.B.J. and M.Ed. from the University of Georgia and is interested in researching two areas: student motivation and issues related to tracking.

Beth Tatum teaches English at Cedar Shoals High School in Athens, Georgia. She has earned a B.S.Ed., M.Ed., and Ed.S. from the University of Georgia and has been recognized by the Foundation for Excellence in Education. She strives to create lifelong learners and is especially interested in researching what happens when teens read a shared text with a parent or adult partner.

Jerelyn Wallace is an English teacher at Oconee County High School in Watkinsville, Georgia. She received a B.A. and an M.Ed. from the University of Georgia and is very interested in continuing to learn about preservice teacher education as a participant in this program.

Jenny Hart White is an English teacher at Hart County High School. She received a B.S.Ed. from the University of Georgia and is very interested in learning more about when and why students read.

Amy Wilbourne teaches English at Washington-Wilkes Middle School in Washington, Georgia. She received a B.S.Ed. from the University of Georgia and served as a career counselor at Russell Middle School. She is currently interested in researching vocational education and the integration of computer technology in the regular classroom.

Index